# TAPPING SCRIPTS

# FOR ENTREPRENEURS

# Disclaimer

The book is for informational purposes only. Neither the publisher nor the author is engaged in rendering professional advice or services to the individual reader. The ideas, procedures and suggestions contained in this book are not intended as a substitute for consulting with your physician. All matters regarding your health require medical supervision. Neither the author nor the publisher shall be liable or responsible for any loss or damage allegedly arising from any information or suggestion in this book.

While the author has made every effort to provide accurate information at the time of publication, neither the publisher nor the author assumes any responsibility for errors or for changes that occur after publication. Further, the publisher does not have any control over and does not assume any responsibility for author or third-party websites or their content.

# Dedication

Dedicated to all solopreneurs, business owners and entrepreneurs everywhere! You got this!

# Acknowledgments

To all my entrepreneurial clients and members.

Love you all.

# CONTENTS

# Chapter 1

## What Is This Book About?

*"Risk more than others think is safe. Dream more than others think is practical."*

- *Howard Schultz*

Hi! Welcome to this book of Tapping Scripts for Entrepreneurs!

Of course, you don't HAVE to be an entrepreneur to read and benefit from this. The Book Title Police won't come and arrest you if you use it and you're NOT an entrepreneur! Promise.

So, what on earth is this book about?

If you're familiar with Tapping then you've probably already figured it out. The clue is pretty much in the title.

If you have no idea what Tapping is, panic not. I'll explain more about it soon.

### Why Have I Written This Book?

In the hundreds of workshops I've run and the multitude of people I've worked one to one with – the BIGGEST concern when it comes to Tapping is *WHAT TO SAY*.

And when people are a bit unsure about something, they tend not to do it. Which means they miss out on the MASSIVE benefits that Tapping brings.

Tapping is obviously my business and I've used – and continue to use – it myself. To move me through the resistances, procrastinations, overwhelms, fears and "stuckness" that plague EVERY entrepreneur.

In business, as in life, mindset is **massively** important. However, mindset is also a <u>conscious mind tool</u>. Most of the reasons for the resistances, procrastinations, overwhelms, fears and "stuckness" are based in SUBCONSCIOUS limiting beliefs and programming.

Trying to clear a subconscious problem with just a conscious mind tool is akin to trying to perform surgery with a blunt butter knife.

My speciality is using Tapping for business. To break through the blocks about money, selling, judgement from other people etc. Entrepreneurship is tough enough without lugging all those around as well.

One day, one of my clients said, *"You should compile a load of Tap Along scripts that people can use"*.

What a fantastic idea! So here it is.

# Chapter 2

## A Bit About Tapping

*"An entrepreneur isn't someone who owns a business, it's someone who makes things happen."*

- *Tim Ferriss*

Look, I'm gonna 'fess up from the start.

TAPPING LOOKS REALLY WEIRD.

But don't be fooled. This is an evidence based technique that reduces stress fast.

Why is reducing stress so very important for an entrepreneur?

Well, it's important for everyone. But when you run your own business and are stressed, you lose focus. You can't see the bigger picture. Your logical brain goes offline. You can be very emotional or frequently ill (a nightmare if you're working on your own). You become reactive as opposed to PROACTIVE.

In layman's terms – **it's a bloody nightmare**.

But, if you had a tool that you could use to reduce your stress response *quickly*, bringing your logical brain back online and taking you out of the spinning wheels of panic…what could you do? How would that change things for you?

I'll give you a little example.

I'd not long ago run a small workshop. There were 152 attendees. Now, I usually have a lady that rings attendees post workshops to find out how they got on – but she was very rudely on holiday.

So, as a small business owner, it fell to me.

And I HATE ringing people (I'm working on that – I know where it comes from). It makes me very uncomfortable. I was running both a STRESS RESPONSE and a LIMITING BELIEF. Both of them fueling each other.

I found myself 'finding other things to do'. My inner voice was running a dialogue along the lines of *just text them, or send an email*. It was super tempting. So, I busted out some Tapping. Just 90 seconds was enough to change the inner dialogue from *I don't want to!* to just fucking do it! So, I did. **And the very first call resulted in a £2k sale.**

Neither that, nor the others, would have happened if I'd just texted. I'd have lost out on a lot of money. And money (or the lack of it) is one of THE biggest stressors!

**How Does Tapping Work?**

So, what IS Tapping and how does it work?

Imagine your brain is like a computer storage system.

Every event in your life is stored in a folder. That folder contains a movie or an image of what happened. An emotion. A physiological reaction. And a decision that was formed in the moment.

Let me give you an example:

As a kiddie, you were asked to present something to the class. As you stood at the front of the classroom giving your presentation, you got something wrong or stumbled over your words. The class laughed at you. Maybe the teacher said something derogatory. You felt shame, embarrassment, humiliation. Your body got sweaty, your face went red, maybe you started shaking. In that moment, you made a decision. That decision might've been to never speak in public again because you look stupid and you're no good at it.

So, you have a movie or image of that event (complete with soundtrack). You have the emotion. You have the physiological reaction. And you have the decision.

That all gets stored in its own folder.

Now, fast forward to present day – you can insert the fluttering of calendar pages if you like.

Your boss approaches you and tells you there's a promotion coming up you'd be excellent for. Loads more money, doing a job of your dreams that will bring you a butt load of fulfillment. Sounds awesome! All you need to do to secure this new position is…

GIVE A PRESENTATION.

As soon as your boss utters those words your brain goes "Ey up! We've encountered that or something similar before and it did NOT go well!" It rifles through the files and finds the one from all those years ago –

and runs it. You may not even consciously remember the event, but your body goes into the exact same reaction it did in the classroom. A feeling of shame, humiliation and embarrassment washes over you. And your inner voice pipes up with "but I'm no good at public speaking!".

One of two things will then happen.

1) You go for it anyway, but you're so stressed and anxious about it that you cock it up entirely and this reinforces the belief you can't speak publicly.

2) You say "no thank you" and walk away from the job of a lifetime.

Neither of these options is good and both leave you feeling like shit.

Tapping acts like a virus scanner to find and release these negative and limiting beliefs and emotions – freeing you to be all you can be.

It also talks directly to the stress centre of your brain and tells it to chill the fuck out – which is why it's so fast and effective at reducing stress.

**How To Tap**

As previously warned, it looks weird. But stay with me cos, whilst it may look a bit silly, it's bloody effective…and simple. I think it's that last part that puts some people off. We do love to over complicate things – and there's a school of thought that if something isn't complicated or hard then it can't really work.

Let's start with the nine basic points:-

## Set Up

*Karate Chop* (fleshy outside edge of hand – the one you'd Karate Kid someone with)

## Round

*Eyebrow* (where your eyebrow starts, near your nose)

*Side Eye* (the outside corner of your eye on the bony eye socket. If you're tapping your temple you've gone too far)

*Under Eye* (under your eye on the bony eye socket)

*Under Nose* (where it says on the tin)

*Chin* (in the groove between your lower lip and chin point)

*Collarbone* (the easiest thing to do here is make a fist and tap where you'd find the knot of a tie)

*Under Arm* (a couple of inches below the arm pit – where a woman's bra strap would be)

*Top of Head* (if you were to draw two lines from the tops of your ears to the top of your head, where they meet is where you tap)

**Please see Figure 1 for a visual.**

You'll have noticed that these have been divided into a Set Up and a Round. I'll go into these in more detail in a minute.

When Tapping, you can you use as many fingers as you want. I tend to use 4 on the Set Up and 2 on the Round.

You can tap on either or both sides of your face and torso. You can swap sides halfway through. The acupressure points you're tapping are on meridian lines and these run equally up and down both sides of your body.

You want to tap hard enough that you can feel it, but not so hard that you end up covered in lots of little bruises.

And that's the mechanics of Tapping. Simples (as a famous meerkat once said).

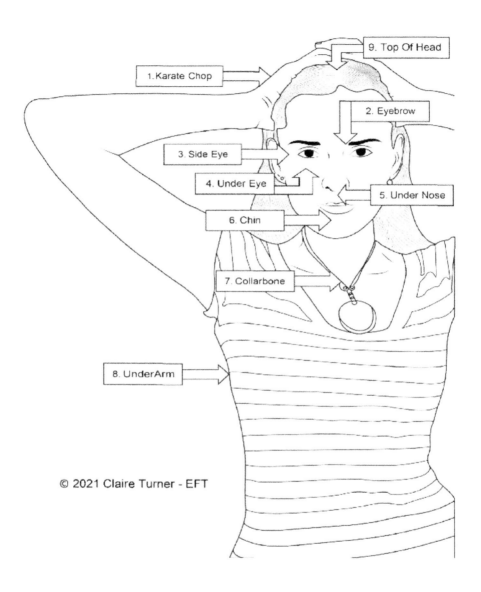

**Figure 1**

Now comes the bit that many people find hard. **The Words**.

Whilst I'm giving you scripts to tap along to, it's important to know the reasoning behind what to say and why.

Let's start by looking at the **Set Up Statement**.

An example of a Set Up statement might be:

*"Even though I'm feeling so stressed, I love and accept myself anyway"*

("Even though [negative/challenge], [acceptance of feeling]")

That last bit might be really hard for you to say, but it's important that you do because it's about accepting how you feel and honouring that.

When you accept how you feel the fight ends, the emotion moves through you and leaves - allowing you to feel something better in its place. What you resist persists…so stop resisting it.

In the case of our earlier example, a simple Set Up statement might be…

*"Even though I have a fear of public speaking, I love and accept myself anyway"*

Or perhaps…

*"Even though I didn't go for that job promotion cos I'm no good at public speaking and now I feel like an idiot, I love and accept myself anyway"*

You repeat the Set Up Statement three times and then move onto a **Round**.

A Round is made up of what are called Reminder Phrases. You're basically just repeating aspects of the Set Up Statement, or anything else that keeps the issue front of mind.

So…*"I'm no good at public speaking; I feel like shit, I get shaky and feel sick when I think about it…"* etc

The whole point of Reminder Phrases is to keep the issue front and centre so it can be worked on.

You'll probably find that, as you tap, memories or thoughts tend to pop up. Make a note of these as they are popping up for a reason and can be worked on later. *Don't dismiss anything that pops up*. Even if it appears to be completely unrelated.

**Negatives**

When Tapping, we concentrate first on the negative issue or emotion. This can worry some people because it sounds like we're tapping in negativity. Actually, the opposite is true. We're bringing the negativity up so we can let it go. As the great Louise Hay once said, *"To clean your house you have to see the dirt"*.

You can of course do 'positive' Tapping, which is great to start your day and gets you in a positive mind space…but if you're looking to release deep rooted negative beliefs then it's a little like polishing a turd. It looks a bit shinier, but the shit is still there. <u>Don't be afraid to get stuck into the negatives</u>.

Yes, you might get a bit emotional…but keep Tapping and the emotion WILL calm down.

In fact, if you are in the middle of feeling the feels you don't even need to speak. It's already front and centre as you're feeling it.

When you've done some 'negative' Tapping, I think it's nice to end with a bit of positive. This can take the form of how you would rather feel: *"I choose to feel happy"*. A word of warning on this though. If *"I choose to feel happy"* has your inner voice making a snarky comment, soften it. Try *"I'm OPEN to feeling happy"*. Why? Whatever your inner voice says is what you end up affirming. This is why so many people think positive affirmations don't work – cos they're not actually affirming the positive. They're affirming whatever their inner voice said at the end. You want your inner voice on board with you.

## Monitoring Your Progress

Tapping is so good that you can forget how bad the thing was beforehand. And that can lead you to think that Tapping doesn't work! So, there are a couple of cunning ways to monitor your progress.

## SUDS

Subjective Units of Distress Scale.

This is a fancy way of saying *'give what you're feeling/believing a number'*.

On a scale of 1 to 10 (where 10 is high or true), how shit do you feel? How true does it feel that you're no good at public speaking?

Go with the first number that pops up and note it down.

After a few Rounds check in with yourself and note what's happened to that number. You're looking for it to have reduced. If it hasn't, keep tapping and get more specific on what's bothering you.

<u>Physical Sensations</u>

So, you feel like shit? Where do you feel that in your body? What colour is it? What texture? How big?

Our body talks to us. We need to listen. Working the physical sensations into the Set Up and the Rounds is really useful and adds extra oomph.

As with the SUDS, after a few Rounds check what's happened to the physical sensation. Is it the same? Changed colour? Changed texture? Moved?

The more you keep track of what's going on, the more in tune with your body and mind you get. And the easier you can see your Tapping progress.

**Releasing**

When you start to release your blocks, a few things can happen.

Yawning.

Burping (my personal favorite).

Tingling sensations.

Tiredness.

Tears.

Temperature changes.

All of this is normal and a great sign. Keep going!

**Find Out More**

I could go on and on about Tapping all day, steadily making it sound more complicated as a result!

I have tried to keep the above as basic and as short as possible but do encourage you to dig a bit more into it.

Before going any further please check out the following link for more information on Tapping.

https://youtu.be/RwEPmOgpJk8

# Chapter 3

## Before Using The Tapping Scripts

*"Success doesn't come from what you do occasionally. It comes from what you do consistently."*

- *Marie Forleo*

As I mentioned before, the main thing people struggle with when they Tap is knowing what to say. That's why I'm about to give you a whole load of scripts for that.

BUT.

That doesn't mean you can sit back and do nothing. Nor does it mean that just *reading* the scripts will solve all your problems.

YOU HAVE TO TAP.

It sounds a little obvious and maybe a touch facetious…but as awesome as Tapping is, it'll only work <u>if you do it</u>. And do it *consistently* for best results.

I also encourage you to, as you start to get the hang of this, try out your own words. In fact, I'm even giving you a *customisable* script for just that.

But the thing that's going to have the BIGGEST impact on your results is not just blindly reading the script whilst tapping the points. It's going to be what you THINK about and what you FEEL as you do so. And the QUESTIONS you ask yourself off the back of that.

So, before you bound off to the scripts section, please go through these questions…

1) How am I feeling right now and how intense is that, 1-10?

2) Where do I feel it in my body and what does it feel like?

3) Why am I feeling like this?

4) Why do I have to feel like this?

5) When did I learn that I had to feel this (or, when does that remind me of)?

6) What belief might be behind that?

7) Is that really true?

8) Who would I be without that belief?

**Beliefs**

The reason you subconsciously resist stuff like success, money, selling etc is because of your subconscious beliefs about those things.

And it's these beliefs that're going to keep you STUCK. So, it's really important that you start to become AWARE of why you behave like you do, make the decisions that you make and how you speak to yourself about those things.

As the great Brad Yates says, *"The extent to which you don't have the thing you want is the extent to*

*which you are resisting it"* and resistance comes from BELIEFS. (That's also true in reverse by the way. Keep getting stuff you don't want?...beliefs again baby.)

You can find your beliefs by looking at what you have/don't have in your life.

By the language you use around something.

By the language your friends and family use.

I'm also going to invite you to think about your RULES. Which are pretty similar to beliefs and are what the beliefs lay down to ensure you don't go off track.

Essentially, why have you convinced yourself it's not safe to have lots of money? Or to be successful?

One of the rules I had was that I wasn't allowed to earn more than my dad, cos if I did, I would make him feel like a failure. I didn't want him to feel like that, so I very carefully and cunningly sabotaged myself to keep me and him safe (cos he might not love me any more if I made him feel like a failure).

At no point has my dad ever said or alluded to this being the case, yet here this rule was. Which leads to an important point...

DON'T EXPECT ANY OF YOUR BELIEFS OR RULES TO MAKE ANY LOGICAL SENSE. CHANCES ARE THEY WON'T. That's why mindset alone is going to struggle cracking them.

## Procrastination

I just want to talk briefly about procrastination.

We have a tendency to really give ourselves a hard time for not just getting on and doing something. It feels like a total mystery as to why we can't take the action we know we need to take. We start "shoulding" on ourselves – *I should be able to just get on with it, I shouldn't be so silly* etc.

I want to make one thing very, VERY clear.

Procrastination is FEAR BASED. That's why you're doing it. So, actually, you're showing yourself masses of self love in attempting to keep yourself safe NO MATTER HOW MUCH YOU TELL YOURSELF OFF FOR IT. It's just that that self love is a little misguided (based on your…you guessed it…beliefs).

There are TWO KEY QUESTIONS you can ask yourself to get underneath *why* you're procrastinating:

1) What's the DOWNSIDE to me taking this action/achieving this thing?

2) What's the UPSIDE to staying exactly where I am?

Now, your knee jerk response to question 1 will probably be *there is no downside*. I'm going to challenge that, cos, if there was no downside, you'd have taken the action/achieved the thing already.

So, hang up your logical brain and have a think about it.

An example may be that *if you post the advert you might get more clients which will mean more money but if you get more money your friends will get jealous and stop hanging out with you.*

Downside.

*If you don't post the advert you probably won't get more clients which will mean you don't get rich and you get to keep your friends.*

Upside.

You can find out more about how to eliminate procrastination with Tapping in my imaginatively entitled course: How To Eliminate Procrastination & Take Action in 4 Easy Steps. Just visit my website for more info.

# Chapter 4

## The Tapping Scripts

*"Ask for help not because you are weak. But because you want to remain strong."*

- *Les Brown*

Each script has a title so you can decide how relevant it is to what you want help with right now. Just pick the one that gets as close as possible.

Before you start, take a breath. Check in with yourself. Rate that feeling or belief 1-10. Notice where it is in your body.

When you've finished, check in again. What's changed?

**What to do if your number doesn't go down...**

First off, it may take more than one go. Don't be afraid to repeat.

Beyond that, there are a few reasons why your number may not shift.

1) <u>You're not being specific enough</u>. Now, obviously, when writing these scripts I didn't know exactly what was going on in your life...so they're a bit general by necessity. If that's the case, hold whatever it is you're going through in your head as you Tap, or change some of the words so it fits better.

27

2) <u>There's a perceived downside to letting the number drop</u>. If your number goes down you might actually take the action! F*CK! Super scary! So, you'll subconsciously sabotage yourself by not allowing the number to drop. If you think that might be the case – as is it (say it as it is). Do a Round or two saying out loud why you might not be able to let the number drop. A great example of this is when people are tapping for anger. There's usually anger around some form of unfairness. So, in your subconscious, if you let go of the anger…does that mean you're condoning what happened? Will someone "get away" with something?

3) <u>Your inner teenager is grunting at you</u>. We all have an inner teenager that does not like to be told what to do. So try a Round of saying stuff like, "you can't make me let it go / I refuse to let this number drop / shan't and won't so there". Go on, unleash the inner teen – if you make yourself laugh all the better!

**What to do if your number goes up…**

First off, you'll probably find that your number will go up then drop. That's fine.

What I'm talking about here is when your number ends up higher than when you started. That's the time to get CURIOUS. What did you say or think about that caused that to peak? Cos that's what you then tap on. And to do that, just talk to yourself about it as you tap through the Round points.

If you find yourself getting very emotional, that's ok. Stop talking and just tap until that reduces enough to feel ok. Remember, Tapping turns off the stress response. A big emotion is just that…so keep tapping. And look, tears are negatively charged ions – so crying is literally releasing the negative emotion. The biggest shifts can come from snotty, ugly crying. Just keep tapping.

**KEY:**

KC  -  Karate Chop

EB  -  Eyebrow

SE  -  Side Eye

UE  -  Under Eye

UN  -  Under Nose

CH  -  Chin

CB  -  Collarbone

UA  -  Under Arm

TH  -  Top of Head

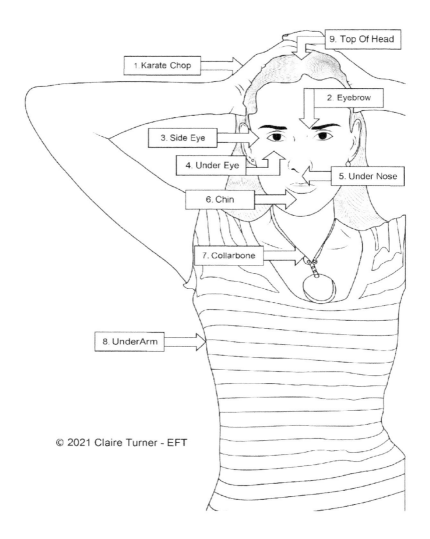

© 2021 Claire Turner - EFT

## Can't Be Arsed!

KC:    Even though I just can't be arsed, I deeply and completely love and accept myself.

KC: Even though I really can't be arsed and I'm really struggling to get going, I deeply and completely love and accept myself.

KC: Even though I just can't be arsed. I would much rather be sat on the sofa watching Netflix. I have so much stuff that I need to do and I really can't be arsed to do any of it. And part of me is feeling really bad about that, but not bad enough to motivate me. And I deeply and completely love and accept myself anyway.

EB:  I cannot be arsed

SE:  I just can't find the motivation

UE:  I'm struggling to get going

UN:  Maybe I've had some time off

CH:  And I've gotten very used to doing nothing

CB:  And now I'm struggling to get back to my routine

UA:  Even if that routine is really good for me

TH:  Even if that routine makes me feel better

EB:  I've gotten so used to doing nothing

SE:  To not making an effort

UE:  And now I'm struggling to pick my life back up

UN:  Perhaps I'm resenting having to pick my life back up

CH:  To having to do stuff that requires effort

CB:  Where I have to engage my brain and deal with problems

UA:  Perhaps the thought of that feels very unsafe

TH:  Feels very unappealing

EB:  Even if I really enjoy doing it when I'm there

SE:  There's a part of me that's just focusing on the effort

UE:     And it's whispering to me.

UN:     "Stay on the couch"

CH:     "Wrap yourself up in a blanket"

CB:     "Go on, pour another glass of wine"

UA:     "Stick Netflix on"

TH:     And there's a very large part of me that wants to listen

EB:     But I know I should be doing something else

SE:     And so there's this battle going on inside

UE:     And I just choose to acknowledge that

UN:     I acknowledge that part of me doesn't want to

CH:     And that's okay

CB:     That part of me is just thinking it's keeping me safe

UA:     It thinks it's doing me a favour

TH:     It's that part that saves me

EB:     When I'm suffering from true tiredness

SE:     It's that part that makes me stop

UE:     When I really, really need to

UN:     And I love and thank that part for keeping me safe

CH:     But it hasn't received the memo

CB:     That I'm feeling better now,

UA:     That it's safe to get back to doing stuff

TH:     And so it keeps running the same program

EB:     I choose to focus on the positives of doing stuff

SE:     The positives of moving my body

UE:     The positives of getting back to work

UN:     I choose to focus on how positive I'd feel

CH:    And I don't have to go all hell for leather at once

CB:    I can choose to do just one thing that moves me forward

UA:    And then I can Netflix for a while

TH:    And I can keep building on that

EB:    I choose to change my language from "should be doing"

SE:    To "want to be doing"

UE:    "Enjoy doing"

UN:    "Choose to do"

CH:    I notice how much better that makes me feel

CB:    How much more excited I feel to get going

UA:    How motivated I feel

TH:    And I choose to take action now

# Clearing Old Shit Before Setting A New Goal

KC:     Even though this backpack is really, really heavy, I can really feel it pulling down on my shoulders full of all the shit that's happened and it feels so uncomfortable, so heavy, I'm open to loving and accepting myself anyway.

KC:     Even though I'm really feeling the heaviness of this backpack, all the goals I haven't hit, all the things I said I'd do and didn't, all the times I told myself I wasn't good enough, all the times other people told me I wasn't good enough. They are like bricks in this backpack and it is so heavy. And I'm open to loving and accepting myself anyway.

KC:     Even though this backpack on my shoulders is so incredibly heavy, I can feel it weighing me  down. It is so heavy and uncomfortable, full of all those things I can't let go of. All those things that are weighing me down and holding me back. And I'm open to the possibility that it's safe to let these things go, and that I can do so easily.


EB:     This backpack is so heavy

SE:     It is so incredibly heavy

UE:     It's really weighing me down

UN:     It's full of all those memories

CH:     It's full of all those limiting beliefs

CB:     It's full of all the mean things My inner voice has said to me

UA:     It's full of all those really painful emotions

TH:     And it is stuffed full

EB:     And I am carrying this backpack around

SE:     And it is so heavy.

UE:     It is so uncomfortable

UN:     It's really weighing me down

CH:     But I have to hold on to all these things

CB:     I have to keep lugging this backpack around

UA:     Even though it's really heavy

TH:     I'm not allowed to put it down


EB:     I've got to keep wearing it

SE:     And it's full of all those times in the past

UE:     Where I did something a bit stupid

UN:     Or didn't do what I said I would

CH:     Or set a goal and didn't achieve it

CB:     And it is weighing me down

UA:     But it's not safe to take it off

TH:     It's not safe to take anything out of it


EB:     It's full of really important lessons

SE:     That I mustn't forget

UE:     But what if I could keep the lesson?

UN:     And let go of the weight?

CH:     What if I could forgive myself?

CB:     What if I could forgive other people?

UA:   What if I could take this backpack off

TH:   And empty out the heavy shit


EB:   Whilst maintaining the lessons

SE:   Which weigh nothing at all

UE:   What if I could feel that bag getting lighter?

UN:   What if I could give myself permission

CH:   To let that bag get lighter

CB:   What if it was safe to put it down

UA:   All those times in the past

TH:   Where I've made a mistake


EB:   Maybe I don't have to keep beating myself up

SE:   All those things that have happened

UE:   That maybe I blame myself for

UN:   Or feel ashamed of

CH:   Or feel guilty about

CB:   Or embarrassed about

UA:   What if I could put those down?

TH:   What if I could take them out of this backpack


EB:   And leave them behind?

SE:   Wouldn't that feel so much lighter?

UE:   Feeling my shoulders feel freer

UN:   Maybe I'm not having to stoop over so much

CH:   Maybe I can feel some energetic shift on my back

CB:    Feel some lightening of my shoulders

UA:    As I give myself permission

TH:    To take that backpack off

EB:    As I give myself permission

SE:    To move forward joyfully

UE:    To move forward with fun

UN:    I'm open to the possibility

CH:    That it's safe for me to do that

CB:    It feels so much lighter

UA:    It feels so much better

TH:    I feel so much freer

EB:    I feel so much happier now

SE:    It feels so much more comfortable now

UE:    This huge weight lifted from my shoulders

UN:    Knowing it's safe to lift the weight from my shoulders

CH:    And it feels really good

CB:    I feel really hopeful

UA:    I feel really motivated

TH:    As I feel light and free

# Confusion and Frustration

KC:    Even though I feel really confused right now, I deeply and completely love and accept myself.

KC:    Even though I feel really frustrated right now, I deeply and completely love and accept myself.

KC:    Even though I feel so confused and even though I feel so frustrated and I really don't like those feelings, it feels really uncomfortable. That's okay. These feelings mean I'm near to a breakthrough and I choose to feel really excited about that. And I choose to allow myself to feel these feelings.


EB:    I'm so confused and frustrated right now

SE:    I feel so confused and frustrated

UE:    And I really don't like how that feels

UN:    Perhaps it makes me feel really stressed

CH:    Perhaps my body is reacting a certain way

CB:    And I'm just so confused and frustrated

UA:    And all I want to do is give up

TH:    I'm sure I'll feel much better if I just give up


EB:    I'm never going to understand this

SE:    It's too hard

UE:    I don't get it

UN:    It makes me feel stupid

CH:    All this confusion

CB:     All this frustration

UA:     I really hate these feelings

TH:     They are so uncomfortable


EB:     I'm never going to understand

SE:     I'm never going to get it

UE:     I might as well just give up

UN:     No!

CH:     Don't give up yet!

CB:     If I can hang in there

UA:     If I can feel excited

TH:     About feeling confused


EB:     About feeling frustrated

SE:     Because these are really good signs

UE:     They mean I'm learning

UN:     They mean I'm about to have a breakthrough

CH:     They mean that my brain is searching for the answers

CB:     It's creating new synapses

UA:     It's creating new neural pathways

TH:     Feeling frustrated and confused is actually a really good thing


EB:     And I allow myself to feel it

SE:     I allow myself to get excited about it

UE:     There's an epiphany in the post

UN:     Very soon it's all going to make sense

CH:    But if I give up now, I'll never know

CB:    If I allow this confusion and frustration to stop me

UA:    Nothing is going to change

TH:    So I choose to feel really good about these feelings


EB:    I choose to feel really excited about these feelings

SE:    I'm going to learn to love feeling frustrated

UE:    I give myself permission to love feeling confused

UN:    Because these feelings are a sign

CH:    I choose to get really excited about that

CB:    I allow myself to feel them

UA:    And to be okay feeling them

TH:    I'm allowing myself to learn and grow

# Fear Of Being Judged

KC:     Even though I'm really afraid of being judged, I deeply and completely love and accept myself

KC:     Even though I'm so afraid of other people judging me. I deeply and completely love and accept myself

KC:     Even though I'm really afraid of what other people will think of me, what they'll say about  me, whether they'll think I'm shit or no good and that's stopping me from doing things. I     deeply and completely love and accept myself, and everybody else involved.

EB:    I'm so afraid of being judged.

SE:    I'm so afraid about what other people will say about me.

UE:    I'm so afraid they'll think I'm shit.

UN:    I'm so afraid they'll think I'm no good.

CH:    I'm so afraid they'll think I'm a waste of space,

CB:    And I can feel this fear in my body,

UA:    And I'm allowing it to stop me doing things.

TH:    I've allowed in the past,

EB:   And I don't want to allow it in the future,

SE:   All this fear about what people will think,

UE:   All this fear about what they say about me.

UN:   I'm too afraid to try,

CH:   Because I'm so afraid of looking stupid,

CB:   Of humiliating myself in public,

UA:   People saying nasty things about me,

TH:   All this fear about being judged.


EB:   And I choose to let that fear go.

SE:   I choose to feel confident.

UE:   I choose to act in spite of this fear.

UN:   Because everybody judges,

CH:   It's inevitable.

CB:   It's a built in human trait,

UA:   Even I judge.

TH:   So of course, others will judge me,

EB:   And I choose to not let that matter,

SE:   Because for everyone judging me badly,

UE:   There's more people judging me goodly.

UN:   I choose to let go of this fear.

CH:   I choose to let go of this fear of being judged.

CB:   It doesn't matter,

UA:   And I'm not going to let it stop me doing what I want to do.

TH:   I choose to know that I'm good enough.


EB:   It doesn't matter what other people think.

SE:   Because the people who really care about me,

UE:   Are much more important than the ones I don't know.

UN:   And yet it's the ones I don't know,

CH:   Whose judgment I fear.

CB:   I choose to let that shit go.

UA:   Fuck them.

TH:   I choose to let this fear go


EB:   Letting it go from every fibre of my being,

SE:     Letting it go from every cell in my body,

UE:     Letting it go all the way back through my past,

UN:     Through those times where people judged me,

CH:     And it hurt,

CB:     And made me afraid of being judged in the future.

UA:     I choose to release all those blocks,

TH:     And I choose to go for and do whatever it is I want.

# Fear Of Failure

KC:   Even though I have a fear of failure, I deeply and completely love and accept myself.

KC:   Even though I have a real fear of failure, I deeply and completely love and accept myself.

KC:   Even though I really fear failure. And because I fear failure, I'm doing an awful lot of      procrastinating because if I don't do it, then I can't fail. I am a genius, but this fear of failure      is now getting really frustrating. It's stopping me achieving what I want to achieve, and I  choose to deeply and completely love and accept myself anyway.

EB:   This fear of failure
SE:   I'm so afraid of failing
UE:   And of what failing will mean
UN:   This fear of failure.
CH:   It's much safer not to even try
CB:   Because if I don't try, then I can't fail
UA:   Genius!
TH:0   If I do try and fail, what will that mean?

EB:   What will it mean about me?

SE:     Is it just more proof that I'm not good enough?

UE:     I'm so afraid of failing

UN:     I'm so afraid of failing

CH:     I'm so afraid of failing, I can't even try

UA:     Maybe.

TH:     Am I really sure it's fear of failure that's stopping me?


EB:     Or is it actually fear of success?

SE:     What will succeeding mean?

UE:     If I try and succeed, what will I have to do?

UN:     What would be the downside of succeeding?

CH:     What would be the upside of failing?

CB:     Maybe I'm just very cleverly convincing myself

UA:     That it's a fear of failure that's stopping me

TH:     Because that sounds a little less bonkers than a fear of
success


EB:     All those times in my past where I've tried and failed

SE:     All those times in my past where I've seen someone else try
and fail

UE:     Did the world end because we failed?

UN:     Or was there a learning experience there?

CH:     Maybe there's more to learn from failing than succeeding

CB:     And maybe that's not necessarily a bad thing

UA:     Would I be as awesome as I am today if I had never failed at
something?

TH:     If I never failed at anything, how would I know when I succeed?

EB:     I have been taught to fear failure

SE:     By people who probably just wanted to try and protect me

UE:     And I'm a really quick learner

UN:     I'm a really good learner

CH:     And I've hung onto this

CB:     I've hung onto this belief that I should fear failure

UA:     When maybe I don't need to

TH:     When I succeed, I celebrate

EB:     I wonder what would happen if I celebrated my failures

SE:     If I celebrated my failures.

UE:     I wonder if I'll be more or less afraid of failing

UN:     I have survived 100% of all my failures

CH:     Maybe I can let go of this fear

UA:     Maybe I could see failure in a whole new light

TH:     What would happen if I chose to embrace failure?

EB:     If I chose to see failure as an opportunity?

SE:     Maybe it's okay to fail

UE:     I can fail fast and I can fail cheap

UN:     And I can learn quickly

CH:     I have survived all my failures

CB:     I am who I am because of my failures

UA:   I am able to help others because of my failures

TH:   It's safe to fail


EB:   I choose to be okay with failing

SE:   I choose to celebrate failing

UE:   I choose to learn from failing

UN:   I choose to learn so I don't keep failing at the same thing

CH:   I allow myself to grow from failing

CB:   I choose to see failing in a whole new light

UA:   I choose to let go of this fear of failure

TH:   I choose to let go of this fear of failure now

# Fear Of Public Speaking

KC:    Even though I'm really afraid of public speaking, I deeply completely accept how I feel.

KC:    Even though I have such a fear of public speaking, I deeply and completely accept how I feel.

KC:    Even though I have all this evidence that I need to be afraid of public speaking, that I'm no good at public speaking, that I can't do public speaking; I deeply and completely accept how I feel. And maybe anyone else who has contributed to this belief.

EB:    I am so afraid of public speaking.

SE:    It scares the bejibiz out of me.

UE:    Even the thought of it makes me sweat,

UN:    Makes me shake,

CH:    Makes my stomach go funny.

CB:    I'm so afraid of public speaking.

UA:    I'm so afraid of standing out.

TH:    I'm so afraid of standing up in front of people.

EB:    The thought of all those faces watching me,

SE:    Is utterly terrifying.

UE:    I need to be afraid of public speaking.

UN:    It's not safe to do public speaking.

CH:    What if I get something wrong?

CB:    What if I stutter?

UA:    What if people laugh at me?

TH:    That would be utterly mortifying.


EB:    And as well as being afraid of public speaking,

SE:    I have this belief that I'm no good at it.

UE:    Maybe there have been times in my past,

UN:    When I couldn't get out of public speaking,

CH:    And the experience was so awful,

CB:    That I vowed to never public speak again.

UA:    I am so scared of public speaking,

TH:    But perhaps it's something I need to do,


EB:    For my work or for my business.

SE:     And part of me wishes I was really good at it.

UE:     I look at all those people who can do it,

UN:     And I think, Wow, they are so brave.

CH:     I could never do that.

CB:     I could never be as brave as them.

UA:     I can never be as good as them,

TH:     Because I'm too scared.


EB:     And whilst I acknowledge this fear,

SE:     It's a very common fear.

UE:     Maybe I don't have to let it rule me.

UN:      People didn't just pop out of their mother's womb.

CH:     Being fantastic public speakers.

CB:     In fact, they couldn't speak at all.

UA:     So maybe this is something that people aren't born with,

TH:     And if they aren't born with it, that means they learned it.


EB:     And if they could learn it, so can I.

SE:     None of the great speakers started out as great speakers.

UE:     They messed up,

UN:     They got things wrong,

CH:     But they kept going.

CB:     They practiced.

UA:     And the more you do something, the easier it gets.

TH:     And even better,


EB:     I can tap before I do it,

SE:     Which will help to calm me down.

UE:     Maybe the fear isn't the fear of speaking.

UN:     Maybe it's more about being judged,

CH:     About what people think.

CB:     Maybe it's about standing out,

UA:     And maybe none of that feels safe,

TH:     But maybe I can do it.


EB:     Maybe the more I do, the better I'll get.

SE:     Maybe I can do a course,

UE:     Maybe I can get training.

UN:    Maybe it's safe to do this.

CH:    Maybe it's safe to grow.

CB:    Maybe it's safe to be seen.

UA:    All those times in the past,

TH:    Where I learned it wasn't safe to do public speaking,

EB:    Where I learned to be afraid of it,

SE:    Maybe I could let emotions and memories go.

UE:    Maybe I could let these limiting beliefs go.

UN:    I can release them from every cell in my body.

CH:    I can release them from every fibre in my being

CB:    And from the energy matrix that surrounds me.

UA:    Maybe those times in the past are just learning opportunities,

TH:    And all that can happen now is that I get better.

# Fear Of Success

KC:   Even though I have a fear of success, which when I say it out loud sounds bloody stupid. That's okay. I deeply and completely love and accept myself.

KC:   Even though I have this fear of success, and it's really stopping me achieving what I want, I can feel myself dragging my heels and procrastinating.

KC:   I deeply and completely love and accept myself anyway. Even though I have this fear of success, and perhaps I don't know where it comes from. Perhaps I can't pinpoint exactly what it is, but I know I have it because I'm stuck. I know I have it because I'm procrastinating, and I choose to release it. I choose to release this fear of success and know that it's safe to be successful.

EB:   This fear of success.

SE:   There's something about success that part of me doesn't find safe.

UE:   And so it's blocking me.

UN:   It's sabotaging me.

CH:   And I'm not doing this to myself because I'm bad or stupid.

CB:     Part of me genuinely thinks it's protecting me,

UA:     And I acknowledge and honor that part of me,

TH:     But I'm going to tell it it's a bit out of date.


EB:     Whatever evidence it's basing this fear of success on,

SE:     Is no longer relevant to me.

UE:     I've moved on. I'm a different person now.

UN:     This fear of success has no place in my life.

CH:     Maybe I got this fear from a specific event.

CB:     Maybe when I've been successful in the past, something bad has happened.

UA:     Maybe someone I loved couldn't handle my success,

TH:     And now I'm afraid that if I'm successful again, I'll lose them.


EB:     Maybe part of me says I shouldn't be more successful than my parents,

SE:     But have I checked with my parents?

UE:     Perhaps I'd be super thrilled if I was super successful.

UN:     Perhaps this belief isn't true.

CH:     Perhaps success is safe.

CB:     I choose to be open to the possibility,

UA:     That it's safe to be successful,

TH:     That it's safe to take the action I need to take,


EB:     And I choose to let this fear of success go.

SE:     I choose to release it from every cell in my body,

UE:     And all the way back through my past,

UN:     To all those times where I perhaps learnt that success was bad.

CH:     Choosing to clear any resistance to success,

CB:     Choosing to feel really excited about being successful,

UA:     Choosing to feel really motivated,

TH:     And choosing to know that it's safe to be successful.

# Feeling Bombarded

KC: Even though I'm feeling completely bombarded by people wanting things, by people demanding answers, I choose to deeply and completely love and accept myself anyway.

KC: Even though I'm feeling completely bombarded and it's making me feel really, really stressed, it's making me feel really anxious, and I deeply and completely love and accept myself anyway.

KC: Even though I'm feeling completely bombarded, bombarded from every direction, and it's putting so much pressure on me and it's making me feel really awful, I deeply and completely love and accept myself anyway.

EB: I'm feeling completely bombarded
SE: It's like the whole world wants a piece of me
UE: Phone calls
UN: Texts
CH: Emails
CB: WhatsApps
UA: It is never-ending
TH: I feel completely bombarded

EB:    I feel under so much pressure

SE:    Everyone wants an answer now

UE:    And if I don't get them their answer immediately

UN:    Or they don't like what the answer is

CH:    They can be absolutely brutal

CB:    They can be so rude

UA:    And that just adds to my sense of stress

TH:    That adds to my sense of anxiety


EB:    It adds to the pressure I feel under

SE:    And it's really upsetting me

UE:    Don't they know I'm trying my best?

UN:    Don't they know how many sleepless nights I have?

CH:    Don't they know how rude they're being?

CB:    Don't care how anxious they're making me?

UA:    Clearly not

TH:    And I feel under such pressure


EB:    I'm close to breaking point

SE:    I just don't think I can take it much longer

UE:    I feel like something is either going to explode

UN:    Or snap

CH:    Or break entirely

CB:    I am under so much pressure

UA:    I am so stressed

TH:    I am so tired

EB:     I am so anxious

SE:     I am so upset by it

UE:     And I really don't want to hear

UN:     How I decide to choose how I feel

CH:     You have no idea how difficult it is

CB:     The levels of pressure I'm under

UA:     The things and people I deal with

TH:     So don't tell me I have a choice


EB:     Because it really doesn't feel like I have

SE:     I cannot see my way out of this pressure

UE:     And maybe that's because I am so stressed

UN:     That there is no blood flowing to my logical thinking brain

CH:     It's all pooling in my arms and legs

CB:     Ready to fight or run away

UA:     I wonder what would happen if I could bring the stress down a little bit

TH:     I wonder what would happen if I could make some time to do that


EB:     But no, I can't make time. I am too busy.

SE:     I'm under too much pressure to make time

UE:     But maybe if I could make the time

UN:     I'd be able to think clearer

CH:     And maybe thinking clearer

CB:   Would make me feel better

UA:   Enable me to do better

TH:   Maybe I could give it a go


EB:   Maybe in the long run it would help me

SE:   I certainly don't want to get to the stage where I snap

UE:   Or break

UN:   Or explode

CH:   It feels like this stress and pressure is out of my hands

CB:   But maybe I can exert some control

UA:   And just take a little bit of time

TH:   To do something like this tap along


EB:   And feel those stress levels come down, even if it's just a little bit

SE:   All this stress

UE:   All this pressure

UN:   All this frustration

CH:   All this anger

CB:   All this anxiety

UA:   I'm really feeling it

TH:   And it feels like utter shit


EB:   I'm open to the possibility I can choose to feel calmer

SE:   I'm open to the possibility I can choose to feel better

UE:   I'm open to the possibility I can take some control

UN:     I'm open to the possibility I can just take a breath

CH:     I'm open to the possibility I can let this overwhelm go

CB:     I'm open to the possibility it's safe to let this pressure go

UA:     I don't need this pressure to perform

TH:     It's safe to let it go now

# Feeling Disappointed

KC:    Even though I'm feeling really disappointed, I am feeling really down that I haven't got this thing or that something didn't happen, and I can feel this disappointment in my body, I deeply and completely love and accept myself anyway.

KC:    Even though I'm feeling all this disappointment, maybe it's like a crushing weight and it's really taken my energy down and it's really upset me. I am so disappointed. And I deeply and completely love and accept myself anyway.

KC:    Even though I'm feeling all this disappointment, and I can feel it right there in my body, and it feels like that, and I know what I'm so disappointed about. I can bring it to mind really easily. And it just feels so bad. I feel so disappointed right now, and I deeply and completely accept how I'm feeling.

EB:    All this disappointment

SE:    I am so disappointed

UE:    I feel utterly crushed

UN:    It's really upset me

CH:    All I can think about is how it could have been

CB:    Or what I could have

UA:    And the fact that I don't.

TH:     Is really upsetting me.


EB:     All this disappointment that I'm feeling.

SE:     It's just dragging my energy down

UE:     I'm so disappointed I could cry.

UN:     Maybe I have been crying already.

CH:     And it just feels so awful

CB:     I am so disappointed

UA:     I am so disappointed

TH:     I got so excited about it


EB:     I'd allowed myself to hope.

SE:     I'd allowed myself to dream.

UE:     And that dream has just been crushed

UN:     So of course I'm really upset.

CH:     All this disappointment right there in my body

CB:     It's almost too much to bear.

UA:     What is even the point in hoping?

TH:     What is even the point in dreaming


EB:     When it's just going to end in disappointment?

SE:     I might as well not even bother.

UE:     So why did I bother?

UN:     Why did I raise my hopes?

CH:     Why did I allow myself to get excited?

CB:     Because what if it went well?

UA:   What if I got what I wanted?

TH:   If I hadn't tried, I wouldn't know.


EB:   And even though right now I feel all this disappointment

SE:   I choose to be open to the possibility.

UE:   That actually it's okay.

UN:   That actually maybe what I thought I wanted

CH:   Isn't entirely true

CB:   Or maybe something even better is on the way

UA:   And if I'd gotten this thing

TH:   I wouldn't have had the room for the better thing


EB:   I give myself permission to feel this disappointment

SE:   It's natural. I don't need to fight it

UE:   I also don't need to live in it

UN:   I give myself permission to feel it

CH:   And I give myself permission to let it go

CB:   I give myself permission to raise my energy

UA:   It's okay to feel disappointment

TH:   There's nothing wrong with it


EB:   And I don't need to stay here

SE:   I give myself permission to feel it and to move on

UE:   Disappointment will happen

UN:   And actually, that's really good

CH:   It shows my energy is high and I'm aiming high

CB:     And that's really exciting

UA:     And I can continue to aim high

TH:     I don't have to let disappointment stop me


EB:     When I was learning to walk

SE:     I fell down quite a lot

UE:     And I got straight back up

UN:     I kept going

CH:     Despite all the disappointment

CB:     Despite all the "failures"

UA:     Despite all the setbacks

TH:     I kept my hope and I kept going


EB:     And look at me now

SE:     Walking about all over the place

UE:     I can even run if I want to

UN:     I choose to feel okay

CH:     I choose to allow hope back into my life

CB:      I choose to raise my energy

UA:     I choose to raise my vibration

TH:     I choose to let go of this disappointment

# Feeling Inspired

KC:    I choose to be inspired and I choose to love and accept myself.

KC:    I choose to feel inspired and I choose to love and accept myself.

KC:    I choose to feel inspired and I choose to feel that motivation and I deeply and completely love and accept myself.

EB:    I choose to feel inspired.
SE:    I choose to feel inspired.

UE:    Inspired to take action,

UN:    Inspired to get things done,

CH:    Inspired creatively.

CB:    I choose to feel inspired.

UA:    I choose to feel that like an energy in my body.

TH:    I choose to feel it energizing me.

EB:    All these inspirational ideas,

SE:    All these inspirational thoughts and feelings,

UE:     I'm choosing to get excited about them.

UN:     I'm choosing to allow that inspiration in.

CH:     I give myself a permission to feel inspired.

CB:     I give myself permission to feel energized by that,

UA:     Releasing any blocks I may be feeling,

TH:     Releasing any resistance to this inspiration.


EB:     I choose to feel inspired.

SE:     I can feel it fizzing away like an energy inside me.

UE:     I'm itching to take action.

UN:     I'm itching to take inspired action,

CH:     Achieving what I want to achieve easily and effortlessly.

CB:     I choose to feel inspired.

UA:     I choose to feel inspired in my whole body.

TH:     I choose to feel really good about that.

# Feeling Nervous About Doing Something

KC:    Even though I'm feeling really nervous, I am feeling really, really scared about doing this, and I can feel it right there in my body, I deeply and completely accept myself anyway.

KC:    Even though I'm feeling really nervous about doing this thing. What if I fuck it up? What if I

look really stupid? What if I get something wrong? I deeply and completely love and accept myself.

KC:    Even though I'm feeling so nervous about doing this, I'm feeling it right there in my body, and my inner voice is going nuts, giving me all sorts of reasons why I shouldn't do it, and it's tying me up in knots, I deeply and completely accept myself anyway.

EB:    I'm really, really nervous

SE:    I really don't want to do this

UE:    But I do want to do it

UN:    It feels really nerve-racking

CH:    I've not really done this before

CB:    I don't really know what I'm doing

UA: It's making me feel really nervous

TH: But it's something I want to do


EB: Maybe it's something that will help other people

SE: Maybe it's something that will uplevel my life

UE: Part of me really wants to take the action

UN: And the other part of me is going, "No!"

CH: What if I look silly?

CB: What if people roll their eyes at me?

UA: What if I get something wrong?

TH: This is a serious business


EB: I have to be very serious about this

SE: I'm not allowed to have fun with it

UE: I'm not allowed to not worry about what people think

UN: And it's making me feel so scared and nervous

CH: And I can feel those nerves in my body

CB: It's almost unbearable

UA: It would be so much easier to just not do it

TH:     And I'd probably feel really relieved for a moment


EB:     But then maybe I'd feel a bit shit

SE:     I'd let it defeat me

UE:     I'd given into my fear

UN:     And so I haven't grown

CH:     I'm still the same

CB:     Only now I'm probably beating myself up about it

UA:     So I'm giving myself a hard time about thinking of doing it

TH:     And then when I talk myself out of it


EB:     I give myself another hard time

SE:     So if I'm going to give myself a hard time no matter what

UE:     I might as well just do it

UN:     And allow myself to feel proud of doing it

CH:     To celebrate that I've done it

CB:     Even if it goes really badly

UA:     Because the great thing is

TH:     I'm going to get goodies no matter what

EB:     It's either going to go really well

SE:     So I get the goodies of feeling awesome

UE:     Or it's going to go a bit off course

UN:     And then I get the goodies of experience

CH:     And I can still choose to feel really awesome

CB:     All this fear that I'm feeling

UA:     All these nerves that I'm feeling

TH:     Feeling them right there in my body


EB:     Holding me back

SE:     Keeping me small

UE:     Stopping me achieving my goals

UN:     Preventing me from helping other people

CH:     Just because I'm worried of looking a bit silly

CB:     Maybe that doesn't matter

UA:     Maybe it's okay to look a bit silly

TH:     Maybe it's okay to just try

EB:    Maybe it's okay to not be quite so serious

SE:    Maybe it's okay to have fun with it

UE:    And that actually feels quite empowering

UN:    Maybe I can give myself permission to just do it

CH:    Maybe I can give myself permission to have fun with it

CB:    Maybe I can allow myself to get a bit excited about it

UA:    Because excitement is just nervousness from the other direction

TH:    And maybe I get to choose which one

# Feeling Scared To Push Your Comfort Zone

KC:     Even though I'm feeling really scared about doing this thing because it's taking me out of my comfort zone, that's okay. I deeply and completely love and accept myself.

KC:     Even though I'm feeling really scared about taking the action I know I need to take because it's going to take me out of my comfort zone and that doesn't feel safe, that's okay. I deeply and completely love and accept myself.

KC:     Even though I'm feeling really scared right now. There's this thing I want to achieve and there's action that I have to take to get it, but they're outside of my comfort zone. And the thought of taking that action is super scary and I'm putting it off. And that's okay. I deeply and completely love and accept myself anyway.

EB:     I'm feeling really scared about taking this action
SE:     I'm feeling really scared about taking this action
UE:     Part of me really wants to achieve the thing
UN:     But the other part of me is going, "No!"
CH:     Because it's going to take me out of my comfort zone
CB:     And that doesn't feel safe
UA:     That feels scary
TH:     And that little voice in my head

EB:    Is giving me all sorts of reasons and excuses

SE:    To not do it

UE:    And part of me wants to believe that little voice

UN:    It feels so much easier to believe the little voice

CH:    But then I won't accomplish the thing

CB:    I won't achieve the thing

UA:    And I really want it

TH:    So I choose to acknowledge the fact that I'm scared


EB:    It's okay to feel fear

SE:    But I'm not going to let it stop me

UE:    I'm going to feel the fear and do it anyway

UN:    I allow myself to step outside of my comfort zone

CH:    And each time I do that

CB:    It's going to feel easier and easier

UA:    Until I'm so used to it

TH:    That it becomes part of my new comfort zone


EB:    And then I can grow

SE:    I can achieve the next thing

UN:    By taking the next step out of my new comfort zone

CH:    I can do it

CB:    I can do it

UA:    Hold my beer!

TH:    Because I'm going for it

EB:    I am brave and courageous

SE:    And I can do this

UE:    And I can keep doing it

UN:    There is no stopping me

CH:    I can do this

CB:    I can take those courageous steps

UA:    And I can keep taking them

TH:    And I allow myself to grow beyond my comfort zone


EB:    I allow myself to keep growing

SE:    Because it's not scary

UE:    It's exciting!

UN:    I allow myself to get excited

CH:    About taking that action

CB:    And all the possibilities that will give me

UA:    I can do this

TH:    And I'm excited about doing it

# How Will I Do It

KC:    Even though I have no idea how to get there, I have this goal that I want to get to, this thing that I want to achieve, but I have no idea how to do it. That's okay. I deeply and completely love and accept myself even though I have this goal. I have this thing I want to accomplish.

KC:    Maybe I told someone I'd accomplish it, but I have absolutely no idea how to do that, and that feels pretty overwhelming. It feels pretty demotivating, and I deeply and completely love and accept myself.

KC:    Even though I haven't got a clue, I have no idea how I can do this. It just seems so big and so overwhelming, I can't even think where to begin. That's okay. I deeply and completely love and accept myself anyway.

EB:    I have no idea where to begin.

SE:    This thing just feels huge.

UE:    And I have no idea where to begin.

UN:    I have no idea how to get this done.

CH:    It just feels completely overwhelming.

CB:     I have this goal that I've set.

UA:     I have this outcome that I want to achieve.

TH:     Maybe I told someone I'd do it.


EB:     And I have no idea how I'm going to do that.

SE:     It's too big.

UE:     There is so much that I have to do,

UN:     That I don't even know where to start.

CH:     And it's really demotivating.

CB:     I don't even want to look at it, let alone do it.

UA:     And I'm allowing this feeling of overwhelm.

TH:     To just stop me in my tracks,


EB:     And I choose to stop that.

SE:     I choose to look at this piece by piece.

UE:     I don't have to do everything all at once.

UN:     I can note down what steps need to happen.

CH:     And if I don't know what steps need to happen,

CB:     I can ask the universe.

UA:    I can ask what steps need to happen.

TH:    For me to accomplish this,

EB:    Because the answers are inside me,

SE:    But at the moment I can't see them,

UE:    Because I'm so overwhelmed by the how.

UN:    So I choose to calm down.

CH:    I choose to take a breath,

CB:    And ask myself the question,

UA:    What do I need to do to accomplish this?

TH:    I could even ask someone else.

EB:    It's okay to ask for help.

SE:    And I could write those steps down one by one,

UE:    Work out which one has to happen first,

UN:    And do that.

CH:    It doesn't all have to be done at once.

CB:    I can break it down.

UA:    I can just concentrate on one step at a time,

TH: And achieve my goal that way,


EB: Because I can do this,

SE: I can achieve this.

UE: I'm feeling overwhelmed and stuck is natural.

UN: It doesn't make me stupid or lazy.

CH: It just looks like it's too much.

CB: So I choose to break it down.

UA: I choose to remain calm,

TH: And I choose to allow myself to tackle it bit by bit.

# I Can Achieve It!

KC:  I choose to know that I can achieve this and I deeply and completely love and accept myself.

KC:  I choose to know that I can achieve this, that I am successful, and I deeply and completely love and accept myself.

KC:  I choose to know that I can achieve this, that I am successful, and I choose to release any blocks or resistance that are perhaps telling me that I can't. And I deeply and completely love and accept myself.

EB:  I choose to know that I can achieve this.

SE:  I choose to know that I am successful.

UE:  I choose to know I can achieve this easily

UN:  Because I'm pretty damn awesome.

CH:  I choose to know that I'm successful

CB:  And I choose to release any little voice.

UA:  That tells me otherwise.

TH:    I choose to release any blocks in the resistance

EB:    To me achieving this.

SE:    To my being successful.

UE:    I choose to let go of any beliefs,

UN:    That were created by past events,

CH:    Times where perhaps I learned

CB:    That I couldn't be successful.

UA:    Perhaps there were times where I didn't achieve something.

TH:    And so I formed the belief that I couldn't be successful.

EB:    Maybe I stopped trying.

SE:    Maybe it didn't feel safe to achieve something.

UE:    Maybe it didn't feel safe to be successful.

UN:    And so I wasn't.

CH:    Because my subconscious is a genius.

CB:    And it's really good at keeping me safe.

UA:    And so it prevented me from being successful.

TH:    It sabotage my efforts to achieve,

EB:   Not because it's bad,

SE:   It was simply acting out of misguided self love.

UE:   And I acknowledge and thank that part of me,

UN:   And I choose to let it know that it's safe for me to be successful.

CH:   I choose to let it know that it's safe for me to achieve things.

CB:   I'm not the same person and it doesn't need to protect me.

UA:   And I choose to know that I can achieve this.

TH:   I choose to feel excited about achieving this,


EB:   And I can achieve this because I am awesome.

SE:   I easily and effortlessly attract success.

UE:   Sometimes I have to ask myself,

UN:   Why do I achieve things so easily?

CH:   Why is it so easy for me to be successful?

CB:   And I choose to know that I am awesome.

UA:   I choose to allow myself to achieve this,

TH:   And I choose to feel really good about it.

# I Don't Know What I Want To Do (Lacking Clarity)

KC:     Even though I don't have any clarity on what I want to do, I deeply and completely love and accept myself.

KC:     Even though I don't have a clear idea of what it is I want to do or achieve, that's okay. I deeply and completely love and accept myself.

KC:     Even though I'm feeling really uncertain. Maybe I'm feeling a bit lost and I just don't have a clear idea. I'm open to the possibility that I can figure this out, that it will come to me and I deeply and completely love and accept myself.

EB:     Even though I can't really see what I want to do
SE:     I just can't get a feel for it
UE:     I hear so many other people talk about it
UN:     About finding their passion
CH:     About having the job they always wanted
CB:     And whilst part of me is really happy for them
UA:     I feel so frustrated that I don't have that
TH:     I don't know what I want to do

EB:     I just know that I'm not happy where I am
SE:     That I can't see a way forward

UE:    I just don't know what I want to do

UN:    Or maybe I do know what I want to do

CH:    But I can't see how to do it

CB:    And I'm finding myself comparing myself to others

UA:    Everyone else seems to have achieved so much

TH:    And here I am just trudging along


EB:    And I'm feeling quite despondent about that

SE:    I'm feeling quite down about that

UE:    I just don't know what I want to do

UN:    I just don't know how to do it

CH:    And I can't see a way forward

CB:    Maybe

UA:    Maybe I have to search a little bit

TH:    Maybe I have to try a few things


EB:    In order to know what I want to do

SE:    Maybe it's like going into an ice cream shop

UE:    I need to try all the flavours to find my favourite

UN:    And I will find it

CH:    It might not be immediately, but I will find it

CB:    Maybe I could consider what I'm really good at

UA:    And then match that against what I really enjoy

TH:    Maybe there are some crossovers I could utilize

EB:    I choose to trust that it will become clear

SE:    That if I keep asking the question

UE:    I will get an answer

UN:    I might have to ask that question many times

CH:    But I will get an answer

CB:    My subconscious will help me with this

UA:    And I might have to try or do some stuff I don't really end up enjoying

TH:    And that's okay


EB:    It's essential that I know what I don't like

SE:    So I can recognize what I do like when it turns up

UE:    And it will turn up

UN:    I choose to feel really optimistic and hopeful

CH:    Letting go of any despondency

CB:    Letting go of comparing myself to others

UA:    Because I have no real idea if they're working their passion

TH:    Where I'm thinking they're all achieving


EB:    Maybe they feel really unsuccessful

SE:    So I choose to stop comparing myself

UE:    To anyone other than me yesterday

UN:    I allow myself to get clear on what I want to do

CH:    I give myself permission to see it

CB:    I give myself permission to feel it and hear it

UA:     I choose to feel confident

TH:     And I choose to know I will gain clarity

# I'm Not Clever Enough

KC:     Even though I'm not clever enough to do this thing, I deeply and completely love and accept myself anyway.

KC:     Even though I don't think I'm good enough to do this thing because I don't think I'm clever enough. I deeply and completely love and accept myself anyway.

KC:     Even though I don't believe that I'm clever enough to do this thing, and I have evidence in the past telling me that I have all these experiences from the past. Maybe I have people from the past telling me I'm not clever enough. And I choose to deeply and completely love and accept myself. And maybe anyone else who has contributed to this belief.

EB:     I'm just not clever enough to do this thing.

SE:     I'm not clever enough to do it.

UE:     This is what I believe,

UN:     And this belief is based on evidence.

CH:     I have learned that I'm not clever enough

CB:     And I've learned it really well

UA:     Despite not being clever.

TH:     Maybe I've been told in the past,


EB:     That I'm not clever enough.

SE:     Maybe I found things like exam is hard.

UE:     Maybe someone called me stupid.

UN:     Whatever it was, I now know that I'm not clever enough.

CH:     What's a relief that is?

CB:     I mean, at least I know I'm not clever enough.

UA:     I'm going to save myself so much heartache by knowing that.

TH:     Because if I know I'm not clever enough,


EB:     And it's not my fault if I get it wrong.

SE:     I got it wrong cause I wasn't clever enough.

UE:     I can stay small because I'm not clever enough.

UN:     I can not try new things because I'm not clever enough.

CH:     I can not expand my business because I'm just not clever enough.

CB:     What a relief that is,

UA:     To know that I'm not clever enough.

TH:     Now I can stay small.


EB:     Now I can stay safe,

SE:     Because I'm not clever enough to do anything else.

UE:     Maybe!

UN:     Maybe I am clever enough.

CH:     Maybe I'm telling myself a genius lie,

CB:     Because part of me is scared,

UA:     Of what it would mean if I was clever enough,

TH:     What I could accomplish if I was clever enough.


EB:     How much success I could have if I was clever enough,

SE:     But I'm not clever enough so I guess we'll never know.

UE:     This belief that I'm not clever enough.

UN:     Part of me has created this belief to keep me safe,

CH:     Because it's scared of what would happen if I realized I was plenty clever enough.

CB:    And I acknowledge and honor that part of me.

UA:    For trying to keep me safe.

`

TH:    But it's misguided love in this case.


EB:    So I choose to let this limiting belief go.

SE:    I choose to know that I am clever enough.

UE:    I didn't get to where I am today by not being clever,

UN:    And perhaps it's not being clever that I'm worried about.

CH:    Perhaps it's fear of what would happen when I realize I am clever.

CB:    And that I can do this.

UA:    And I choose to release any fear around this.

TH:    I choose to release any blocks around this.


EB:    I release them from every cell in my body,

SE:    And all the way back through my past,

UE:    To all those times I got the idea,

UN:    That I wasn't clever enough.

CH:    I choose to feel really good about myself.

CB:    I choose to feel really good about the fact that I'm awesome.

UA:    I choose to know that I am good enough.

TH:    I choose to know that I am clever enough, and that it's safe to be.

# Lacking Motivation

KC:   Even though I have zero motivation right now, I've got loads to do and I just can't be arsed to do any of it, and that's okay. I deeply and completely love and accept myself anyway.

KC:   Even though I am completely lacking motivation. I have a list of jobs I need to do, and maybe I'm feeling a little bit of overwhelm in there as well, and that's okay. I deeply and completely love and accept myself.

KC:   Even though I have all these things I should be doing, and I've spent most of my day shoulding over myself, but I just feel like I'm lacking the motivation, and that's okay. I deeply and completely love and accept myself anyway.

EB:   I have no motivation
SE:   I have absolutely zero motivation
UE:   I just can't bring myself to do anything
UN:   And there's so much I should be doing
CH:   And I just can't seem to summon the motivation
CB:   For whatever reason, part of me doesn't want to do it
UA:   And I have no motivation as a result
TH:   So why doesn't that part want me to get on with it?

EB:    Why am I procrastinating?

SE:    What's stopping me from getting on with it?

UE:    Maybe it's overwhelm

UN:    Maybe it's fear of some description

CH:    Maybe I just need a break

CB:    Maybe I need to stop shoulding all over myself

UA:    If I've been working really hard

TH:    Maybe this is my body telling me to take a break


EB:    And I can do that.

SE:    I give myself permission to do that

UE:    In this instance though

UN:    I've just had a weekend off

CH:    I've had my break

CB:    And now I'm struggling to get back into it

UA:    And although part of me is saying, "I don't know why"

TH:    I do know


EB:    Maybe I can't bring it to mind right now

SE:    But it's there in my unconscious

UE:    Maybe I enjoyed my break too much

UN:    If there is such a thing

CH:    And there's something about the work I need to do

CB:    That I am resisting at some level

UA:    I choose to acknowledge and accept that

TH:    It's okay to feel like this


EB:    And because I acknowledge and accept it

SE:    I can now let it go

UE:    I can let go of this laziness

UN:    I can let go of this resistance

CH:    I allow myself to get excited

CB:    I allow myself to get organized

UA:    I allow myself to do the things I need to do

TH:    I allow myself to get motivated


EB:    I choose to feel this motivation rising inside of me

SE:    I choose to focus on the good stuff

UE:    That doing this work will give me

UN:    I choose to feel really excited

CH:    I choose to get going with it

CB:    I allow myself to get really motivated

UA:    I allow myself to get my jobs done with ease

TH:    And I choose to feel really energized about it

# Making Time

KC:    Even though I just don't have enough time to do all these things, that's okay. I deeply and completely love and accept myself.

KC:    Even though I'm struggling to find the time to get these things done, that's okay.

KC:    I deeply and completely love and accept myself. Even though I just don't have the time to get all these things done, that's okay. I deeply and completely love and accept myself anyway. And anything else that is contributing to this feeling.

EB:    Just don't have enough time.

SE:    There's all these things I have to do.

UE:    I just don't have the time to do them.

UN:    I can feel them melting up behind me.

CH:    And I just don't have the time.

CB:    I'm afraid they'll never get done.

UA:    Because I don't have enough time.

TH:     All these things I feel I should do.


EB:     The reality is,

SE:     The things are really important to me.

UE:     I make the time.

UN:     Maybe I do that by scheduling it in my calendar.

CH:     Maybe I do that by setting alarm reminders.

CB:     However I do it.

UA:     The things that are really important to me,

TH:     I make the time to do them.


EB:     So maybe I should take a look at this long list of things,

SE:     This long list of things I feel I should be doing.

UE:      And work out which ones are really important,

UN:     Work out which ones will move me forward,

CH:     And then schedule doing those into my day.

CB:     And the other items that I don't feel are as important,

UA:     Or that I don't feel excite me,

TH:     And just aren't urgent.

EB:    Maybe I need to think about crossing them off my list.

SE:    Because they're just going to sit there.

UE:    Yeah, taking up mental RAM in my mind,

UN:    Just hovering over my shoulder.

CH:    And I don't need that.

CB:    Because it distracts me from the important things.

UA:    So maybe I can look at my list,

TH:    And choose the important things,


EB:    So that I can schedule them.

SE:    And the less important things,

UE:    Maybe I can consider getting rid of them,

UN:    So they're not sitting there on my mental shelf,

CH:    Freeing me up

CB:    To think about the things I really want to do.

UA:    The things that I choose to make time for,

TH:    And I choose to make that time.

EB:   I give myself permission to make that time.

SE:   And I also give myself permission,

UE:   To let the less important stuff go.

UN:   I choose to free myself up.

CH:   I choose to move myself forward.

CB:   I choose to schedule those important things into my day,

UA:   Because what gets scheduled gets done,

TH:   And I choose to make that time.

# Not A Serious Business

KC: Even though I don't believe I'm a real business, I deeply and completely accept myself.

KC: Even though I don't believe I'm a real business because I'm not an accountant, I'm not a banker, I'm not a solicitor. I'm something a bit more alternative, and that's okay. I deeply and completely accept myself.

KC: Even though I don't believe I'm a real business, and because of that, I shouldn't be taken seriously. What I'm doing isn't real business stuff, and I don't believe that I should be taken seriously, and I don't believe others do take me seriously. And that's okay. I deeply and completely accept myself. And maybe anyone else who has contributed to this belief.

EB: I don't believe I'm a real business.

SE: I don't believe I'm a serious business.

UE: Other people don't take me seriously.

UN: I they think I'm just playing at something.

CH:     But who says you can't play at work?

CB:     Who says you can't have fun at work?

UA:     Where did that idea come from?

TH:     This belief that I'm not a serious business.


EB:     It's almost got me apologizing for it.

SE:     Perhaps I feel I have to justify it.

UE:     Perhaps I feel I have to play it down.

UN:     Because this isn't a real business.

CH:     It's far too out there.

CB:     It's far too arty.

UA:     And everyone knows arty businesses aren't serious.

TH:     Don't they?


EB:     No one will take me seriously.

SE:     No one will take my business seriously.

UE:     And that stops me taking it seriously.

UN:     And I choose to knock that off.

CH:     There's no reason why this can't be a serious business.

CB:     The arts can be a serious business.

UA:     Crafting can be a serious business.

TH:     Alternative things can be a serious business.


EB:     And no one has the right to tell me otherwise.

SE:     There are many examples of things like this being a serious business.

UE:     If there's an audience, there's a business.

UN:     And just because some people might not think it's serious,

CH:     It's just because they're not in possession of the facts.

CB:     And they're entitled to their wrong opinion.

UA:     But I choose not to let that affect how I feel about my business.

TH:     I choose to believe in my business.


EB:     My passion can be a serious business.

SE:     It can even be a fun business.

UE:     There's no law that business has to be serious.

UN:     There are no business police or come and arrest me if I'm not serious.

CH:     This is my passion and I love it.

CB:     Why shouldn't I make money out of it?

UA:     I choose to release this belief.

TH:     That what I'm doing is not a serious business.

EB:     I'm not going to listen to all those people.

SE:     Who treat me as if I'm less than a serious business.

UE:     They're just jealous that I'm having fun doing what I do.

UN:     I choose to let go of this belief that I can't be a serious business.

CH:     I choose to let go of this doubt in myself and my business.

CB:     I have a gift to give.

UA:     I'm not going to let the thoughts of others stop me.

TH:     I'm not going to let what other people say keep me small.

EB:     I can do this.

SE:     I might need help in some cases, but I can do this.

UE:     I choose to let go of any shame I have about my business.

UN:     I choose to let go of any embarrassment I have about talking about it.

CH:    And I choose to feel proud.

CB:    I choose to feel successful

UA:    Because I am doing what I love

TH:    And not many people can say that. So I choose to feel proud and I choose to feel successful.

# Not Good Enough Low Self Esteem

KC:   Even though I don't think I'm good enough, I choose to be open to loving and accepting myself.

KC:   Even though I don't think I'm good enough, I choose to be open to loving and accepting myself just as I am.

KC:   Even though I don't think I'm good enough. Maybe that's a decision I've made or maybe it's down to something someone's told me. I just know that I'm not good enough. I know that I have low self-esteem and I choose to be open to loving and accepting myself anyway.

EB:   I'm not good enough
SE:   I'm just not good enough
UE:   I don't have much self-esteem
UN:   I don't think I'm worthy or deserving
CH:   I'm making myself very small
CB:   Because I'm not good enough to be anything else
UA:   I'm not good enough
TH:   I have all this evidence in my past

EB:   That I'm not good enough
SE:   All those times where I learnt

UE:  I wasn't worthy or deserving

UN:  And whilst I tell myself I'm not good enough

CH:  One thing I'm really good at

CB:  Is believing that I'm not good enough

UA:  Maybe it doesn't feel safe to be good enough

TH:  If I'm good enough for whatever it is


EB:  What will I have to do?

SE:  If I know that I am worthy and deserving

UE:  What will I have to stop tolerating

UN:  If I made the decision that actually I am good enough

CH:  What is the downside of that

CB:  I'd probably have to do something outside of my comfort

zone

UA:  And that feels more uncomfortable

TH:  Than not feeling good enough


EB:  When did I decide that I wasn't good enough?

SE:  And good enough at what specifically?

UE:  Who told me I wasn't good enough?

UN:  And how did they know?

CH:  Where's my evidence for not being good enough?

CB:  Maybe I have lots of it

UA:  But maybe I have lots of evidence

TH:  Because I will find things that support my belief

EB:     What if I changed my belief?

SE:     What if I was open to the possibility

UE:     That actually I'm plenty good enough

UN:     For instance, no one can be me better than me

CH:     I am energy

CB:     I am part of this universe

UA:     That's evidence that I am good enough

TH:     If I truly wasn't good enough


EB:     Would I even be here?

SE:     I choose to be open to the possibility

UE:     That I don't really believe I'm not good enough

UN:     More, that I am afraid of how good I actually am

CH:     I am good enough

CB:     There may be stuff I can't do

UA:     That doesn't mean I'm not good enough

TH:     All skills are learnable


EB:     I'm open to the possibility I am good enough

SE:     I choose to turn up the volume on my self-esteem

UE:     And only I can do it

UN:     Only I have access to my self-esteem button

CH:     Up till now

CB:     I have chosen to set it low

UA:     For whatever reason

TH:     Perhaps to keep myself safe

EB: That's no longer working for me

SE: I don't want to keep this low self-esteem

UE: Only I can choose to turn it up

UN: I allow myself to focus on all the good bits of me

CH: I allow myself to feel gratitude for everything I have

CB: I choose to reach out and turn up my self-esteem

UA: I give myself permission to do that

TH: And I choose to feel really good about doing it

# Open & Ready To Receive

KC:    I choose to be open and ready to receive, and I choose to deeply and completely love and accept myself.

KC:    I choose to be open and ready to receive, and I choose to deeply and completely love and honour myself.

KC:    I choose to be open and ready to receive all the wonderful things the universe is sending my way. And I allow myself to see and recognize these things, and I align my energy accordingly. And I choose to deeply and completely love and accept myself.

EB:    I choose to be open and ready to receive
SE:    I choose to be open and ready to receive
UE:    I allow myself to be open and ready to receive
UN:    All the good stuff the universe is sending my way
CH:    As well as all the learnings it's sending to me
CB:    Although it may not feel like it
UA:    Sometimes the learnings can be even more important than the good stuff
TH:    I choose to be open and ready to receive

EB:    I allow myself to focus on what I want
SE:    I acknowledge the universe is working with me

UE:     Supporting me

UN:     Wanting me to succeed

CH:     And I choose to help it do so

CB:     I choose to be open and ready to receive

UA:     I choose to allow the magic of the universe

TH:     Into my life


EB:     And to do this, I choose to be open and ready to receive

SE:     Whatever that may mean to me

UE:     Allowing myself to focus on what I want

UN:     Allowing myself to feel what having that will feel like

CH:     Giving myself permission to be open and ready to receive

CB:     Allowing myself to feel optimistic and happy about it

UA:     Allowing myself to take the necessary action

TH:     Allowing my body and my energy to be open and ready to receive

# Overwhelmed

KC:     Even though I'm feeling really overwhelmed right now. I love and accept myself

KC:     Even though I'm feeling so overwhelmed right now. Maybe because I don't know how to do it, and so I'm feeling really, really overwhelmed about it. Maybe it's an emotion. Maybe I'm feeling overwhelmed by a certain emotion and that's okay. Right here, right now, I'm okay.

KC:     Even though I'm feeling so overwhelmed right now. There's so much I have to get done. My to-do list is the longest in the world and it's making me feel really overwhelmed. Maybe because I don't have the time. Maybe because I don't know where to start. And I deeply and completely love and accept myself. And maybe anyone else who is contributing to this feeling of overwhelm.

EB:     I'm feeling so overwhelmed.

SE:     There's just so much to do.

UE:     There's just so much emotion.

UN: I don't have the time to do everything.

CH: I don't have the capacity to deal with this emotion.

UA: And I'm feeling really overwhelmed.

TH: And I can feel that in my body.


EB: It's just swamping me.

SE: Maybe it feels like I'm drowning.

UE: I'm just so overwhelmed right now.

UN: And I can't see a way out of it.

CH: I can't see how to get out of this overwhelm.

CB: And that's overwhelming.

UA: I'm being overwhelmed by overwhelmed.

TH: And it's not feeling good.


EB: I feel like I have so much to do.

SE: Maybe I feel that people are depending on me.

UE: All this emotion that I'm feeling.

UN: And I just can't cope with it.

CH: I am feeling so overwhelmed.

UA:     I am feeling so overwhelmed

TH:     And I just can't seem to get out of it.


EB:     What if there was a way I could feel better?

SE:     What if there was something I could do to feel better,

UE:     To calm this overwhelmed down?

UN:      If only there was a way.

CH:     Oh wait, I'm doing it.

CB:     I have this amazing tool called tapping.

UA:     And I can use it whenever I need to.

TH:     To get myself out of this stress response.


EB:     To calm this overwhelmed down.

SE:     And when I'm feeling calm,

UE:     I can access the answer to whatever the question is.

UN:     When I am calm, I can do that.

CH:     And tapping is so good at calming me down.

CB:     So I choose to tap when I need to.

UA:     I choose to be proactive.

TH:     And to take back control from this overwhelm.


EB:     Because I'm a smart cookie.

SE:     But when I am in a stress response,

UE:     I just can't access it.

UN:     So I choose to calm myself down.

CH:     I choose to let go of this overwhelmed feeling.

CB:     I choose to take back control.

UA:     And to feel better about this.

TH:     In every way possible.

# Pure Potential

KC: I am pure potential and I choose to feel really good about that.

KC: I am pure potential and I choose to feel really excited about that.

KC: I am pure potential. Anything and everything is possible and I choose to allow myself to feel really excited about that. I choose to allow myself to feel really good about that. And I choose to be open to exploring my full potential.

EB: I am pure potential

SE: I am pure potential

UE: And that's a really exciting thought

UN: Because if I'm pure potential

CH: Anything is possible

CB: If I'm pure potential

UA: Which I absolutely am

TH: I can achieve anything I want to

EB: I feel really excited about this

SE: It is really exciting

UE: I am pure potential

UN:    And I feel really good about that

CH:    Because if I'm pure potential

CB:    I have the potential to manifest whatever I want

UA:    And if I have any little doubting Thomas voice in my head

TH:    About the fact that I am pure potential


EB:    I choose to let that voice go

SE:    Because I am pure potential

UE:    I am made up entirely of energy

UN:    Everything around me is made up of energy

CH:    All that energy is interconnected

CB:    All that energy is linked

UA:    Which means that I am pure potential

TH:    It means I can shape my energy


EB:    It means I can attract whatever I want into my life

SE:    Letting go of any blocks that might prevent that

UE:    Blocks from past events

UN:    Blocks from other people

CH:    All those times where I might have learnt

CB:    That I was less than full potential

UA:    That I was less than pure potential

TH:    I choose to release those blocks now


EB:    From every cell, muscle, and fibre of my body

SE:    Releasing them from my energy field

UE: Releasing them from my timeline

UN: Releasing them from the past, present, and future

CH: Acknowledging and allowing my pure potential

CB: Feeling really good about my pure potential

UA: Feeling really excited about my pure potential

TH: I am pure potential

# Resistance To Doing Or Achieving Something

KC:     Even though I have all this resistance, I deeply and completely love and accept myself.

KC:     Even though I have all this resistance to doing the thing, to achieving the thing. I deeply and completely love and accept myself.

KC:     Even though I have all this resistance, perhaps I can feel it in my body. Perhaps this resistance is due to a limiting belief. Perhaps it's because I don't know how to do the thing, or perhaps there's something that I'm subconsciously afraid of. And that's okay. I deeply and completely love and accept myself and anyone else who is contributing to this resistance.

EB:     All this resistance.

SE:     All this resistance.

UE:     I know what I should be doing

UN:     But I find myself doing all sorts of other things instead.

CH:     This resistance that I'm feeling

CB:    To doing something

UA:    To achieving something

TH:    Something is stopping me.


EB:    I can feel this resistance in my body.

SE:    I have become the procrastination queen - talking.

UE:    All this resistance.

UN:    And part of me really wants to achieve this thing.

CH:    Part of me really wants to do this thing,

CB:    But there's another part of me that's saying nope.

UA:    And that's the part that's throwing up the resistance.

TH:    And since we only ever do things for our own good,


EB:    There must be something about doing this thing.

SE:    There must be something about achieving this thing.

UE:    That feels unsafe to some part of me.

UN:    Otherwise I'd already have it.

CH:    Otherwise I'd already have done it.

CB:    Instead, I have this resistance.

UA:    So what would be the downside of achieving this thing?

TH:    What would be the downside of doing this thing?


EB:    Because it's fairly unlikely.

SE:    That it will risk life and limb.

UE:    So we are talking a perceived danger.

UN:    My subconscious is perceiving danger

CH:    Where actually no danger exists.

CB:    So what would be the downsides of achieving it?

UA:    What would be the downsides doing it?

TH:    What are the upsides of not doing it?


EB:    What are the upsides of not achieving it?

SE:    Or this resistance?

UE:    Maybe I can let it go.

UN:    Maybe the perceived danger is just that.

CH:    Of course, if it's real danger, maybe I need to rethink it.

CB:    All this resistance.

UA:    All this belief that it's keeping me safe.

TH:     I choose to let it go.


EB:     I choose to know it's safe to do the thing.

SE:     I choose to know it's safe to achieve the thing.

UE:     I choose to let go of any limiting beliefs that suggest otherwise.

UN:     I let them go from every cell in my body.

CH:     I let them go from the energy that surrounds me.

CB:     I let them go all the way back through my past.

UA:     Through all those times it taught me it wasn't safe.

TH:     And I choose to clear out this resistance now.

# Attacked Online

KC:     Even though I feel really angry about what just happened, I deeply and completely love and accept myself.

KC:     Even though I feel really upset by what they said to me. It was an extremely personal attack. And of course, I'm upset by it. And I deeply and completely love and accept myself anyway.

KC:     Even though I'm really upset by this. I feel really shaky. Perhaps I've had trouble sleeping. And I just keep replaying it In my mind. I'm angry by the injustice of it. Who the fuck do they think they are? How dare they talk to me like that? I am really angry. I'm really upset. And perhaps it's made worse because I can't really do anything. I'd like to bop them on the nose, but it's on the internet and it just feels like I can't do anything. And I deeply and completely  love and accept myself anyway.

EB:     I'm really fucking angry
SE:     They have really upset me
UE:     And they don't even bloody me
UN:     How dare they write those things?
CH:     How dare they make me feel this way?
CB:     Who the fuck do they think they are?
UA:     Oh, I am so fucking angry about it

TH:     That was a really personal attack

EB:     For absolutely no reason

SE:     It was really vicious

UE:     And as much as it's made me angry

UN:     It's also really upset me

CH:     It feels so unfair

CB:     It was such a personal attack

UA:     And I can't stop thinking about it

TH:     It's really getting to me

EB:     And perhaps that's making me angry too

SE:     That this small-minded little person

UE:     Has been able to upset me so much

UN:     And logically, I know it says more about them

CH:     But logic doesn't really have a say here

CB:     They have made me feel very unsafe

UA:     They've made me feel unsafe emotionally

TH:     And it's really upset me

EB:     And it's upset me that I've allowed it to upset me

SE:     Of course, it's upset me

UE:     I'm human, not a robot

UN:     And what they said really hurt

CH:     And I really want to defend myself

CB:     And perhaps I did defend myself

UA: And It just made everything worse

TH: I'm so upset by this

EB: My heart is racing

SE: I feel really shaky and trembly

UE: Because my body has gone into a stress response

UN: And it feels really emotional

CH: And perhaps I'm lying awake at night, stewing over it

CB: And it scared me

UA: It's hard enough getting out there and being seen

TH: Particularly if I'm trying to sell something

EB: And this has really knocked me

SE: It's knocked my confidence

UE: And it's made me afraid

UN: Well, fuck that

CH: I will not allow this small-minded person

CB: Such power over me

UA: Bollocks to that

TH: I refuse to let them beat me down

EB: I know I'm a good person

SE: I will not allow them to sway me.

UE: They have no idea what I'm going through

UN: They have no idea what I deal with

CH: Just as I have no idea what they're going through

CB:    There is no excuse for what they did

UA:    But how much pain do you have to be in to do that?

TH:    To strike out like that for no reason


EB:    How unhappy and insecure do you have to be

SE:    To do something like that to someone else

UE:    What they did was wrong

UN:    But by allowing myself to carry that around

CH:    I am doing exactly what they want me to do

CB:    I am giving them power over me

UA:    Well, fuck that shit

TH:    I refuse to give them power over me


EB:    I choose to allow myself to let this go

SE:    I'm open to the possibility.

UE:    That I can't hold onto this tight enough

UN:     I can't feel upset enough

CH:    To change what happened

CB:    But what I can do is let it go.

UA:    I don't have to let it go all at once

TH:    There's probably some part of me that wants to hang on to it


EB:    That wants to remain outraged

SE:    Because letting it go feels like I'm forgiving them in some
way

UE:    That I'm condoning what they did

UN: That I'm just rolling over and taking it

CH: But that's the thing, I'm not taking it

CB: I'm not even picking it up

UA: They are looking for a reaction

TH: So I'm not going to give them one


EB: I'm open to the possibility

SE: That I am powerful enough to let this go

UE: I choose to be the calm, confident person I know I am

UN: And that little person can't hurt me

CH: At least not for long

CB: I choose not to let them

UA: I will not let what they said ruin my day

TH: Because I know I'm better than that


EB: I choose to be calm

SE: I choose to be confident

UE: I choose to let it go

UN: I choose to be powerful

CH: I choose to be stoppable

CB: I choose to let it go

UA: I choose to be awesome

TH: I choose to let this go and feel good

# FEELING CONFUSED

KC:     Even though I'm feeling really confused, I deeply and completely love and accept myself

KC:     Even though I'm feeling really confused by all this, I choose to deeply and completely love and accept myself

KC:     Even though I'm feeling really confused, my brain doesn't get it, it's all new – that's OK. I deeply and completely love and accept myself anyway

EB:     I'm feeling really confused about all this

SE:     It's too much to take in

UE:     I don't get it

UN:     It's all new to me

CH:     There's so much to get my head around

CB:     It's seems really complicated

UA:     I feel like I'm never going to understand it

TH:     It's all just too confusing


EB:     I've never done this before

SE:     It's new to me

UE:     It's confusing the hell out of me

UN:     I can't believe it really works

CH:     It's all a bit weird and woo woo

CB:     It seems to simple to work

UA:     So simple it's confusing

TH:     I'm feeling really confused


EB:     And that's frustrating

SE:     I want to understand it instantly

UE:     I'm frustrated by my confusion

UN:     It makes it all more confusing

CH:     It's too difficult to work out

CB:     It's too difficult to get my head round

UA:     It's harshing my happy

TH:     Part of me wants to just give up

EB:   It would be so easy to just give up

SE:   Because it feels too confusing

UE:   Too frustrating

UN:   Too difficult

CH:   But maybe confusion could be the new learning

CB:   Perhaps this feeling of confusion

UA:   Is my brain's synapses

TH:   Trying to make a connection


EB:   And the confusion and frustration

SE:   Is because that connection is so close

UE:   Those synapses are almost touching

UN:   And when they do touch

CH:   That's when understanding happens

CB:   Perhaps this feeling of confusion

UA:   Is actually a really good sign

TH:   A sign that I'm about to learn and understand

EB:    If I give up now I'm denying myself that learning

SE:    If I can just stay in the confusion for a little while

UE:    If I can stay in the frustration a little while

UN:    I will be rewarded with learning

CH:    With understanding

CB:    And that will feel so good

UA:    That will really help my happy

TH:    It will be an achievement


EB:    I choose to relax into this confusion

SE:    And trust that understanding will come

UE:    I choose to relax into this frustration

UN:    And trust that understanding will come

CH:    I choose to give it a go

CB:    I choose to see confusion as an exciting sign

UA:    I choose to feel good about confusion

TH:    I choose to feel excited about feeling confused

# NOTHING TO FEEL GRATEFUL ABOUT

KC:   Even though I don't think I have anything to feel grateful about, I deeply and completely love and accept myself

KC:   Even though I don't think I have anything to feel grateful about, I deeply and completely love and accept myself

KC:   Even though I don't think that I have anything to feel grateful about and that really brings me down and perhaps makes me feel ungrateful, I deeply and completely love and accept myself.

EB:   I have nothing to feel grateful about

SE:   I really don't think I have anything to feel grateful for

UE:   And that feels really bad

UN:   That makes me feel sad

CH:   And perhaps ungrateful

CB:   Perhaps I'm even feeling sorry for myself

UA:   Perhaps I'm feeling envious of others

TH:     All these other people who have more to feel grateful for than me

EB:     All these other people who are so much better off than me

SE:     Who have more than me

UE:     They have loads to be grateful for

UN:     I have nothing to feel grateful for

CH:     There is nothing in my life that I can feel grateful for

CB:     Not the air that I breathe

UA:     Not the fact that I can read this book

TH:     Not the fact that I can afford this book

EB:     I have nothing to feel grateful for

SE:     I have nothing to be grateful for

UE:     And being told to feel grateful

UN:     Is not making me feel any better

CH:     It's like when I was young

CB:     And someone would give me a gift

UA:     Before I could even begin to feel grateful

TH:    A parent said to me


EB:    "And what do we say?!"

SE:    I was told to feel grateful

UE:    Before I could naturally feel grateful

UN:    And perhaps younger me really resented that

CH:    Resented being told to be grateful

CB:    Resented being told to write thank you letters

UA:    And so now I'm determined to not be grateful

TH:    And I can't be grateful


EB:    If I have nothing to be grateful for

SE:    I'm such a genius

UE:    By not allowing myself

UN:    To see all the blessings in my life

CH:    I am relieving myself

CB:    Of having to feel grateful

UA:    And that's working out really well for me

TH:    Maybe

EB:     Maybe if I allowed myself to feel grateful

SE:     I wouldn't have had to buy a book on being happy

UE:     Maybe there are more blessings in my life

UN:     Than I can possibly imagine

CH:     They may not be big, expensive things

CB:     But they are still little miracles in their own right

UA:     My heart is beating

TH:     I have air I can breathe


EB:     And that doesn't sound like much

SE:     But it becomes important very quickly

UE:     If there is no air to breathe

UN:     Maybe it's all about perspective

CH:     Maybe the more I find to be grateful for

CB:     The more there IS to be grateful for

UA:     I can read – many others can't

TH:     I can afford this book

EB:    Many others can't

SE:    I have access to food

UE:    Many others don't

UN:    There's actually so much to feel grateful for

CH:    I allow myself to find things to feel grateful for

CB:    I give myself permission to feel grateful

UA:    Not because I have to or have been told to

TH:    But because I choose to

# FEELING A BIT SILLY

KC:   Even though I feel a bit silly doing this, I choose to be OK with it

KC:   Even though I feel a bit silly doing this, I choose to love and accept myself anyway

KC:   Even though I feel a bit silly and I'm worried what other people may think about me, I choose to love and accept myself anyway – and maybe everyone else whose judgement I fear

EB:   I feel a bit silly

SE:   I feel a bit silly doing this

UE:   What must I look like

UN:   What would other people think

CH:   I feel a bit silly

CB:   And that bothers me

UA:   I mustn't look silly

TH:   It's not safe to look silly

EB:   It's not safe to be silly

SE:   People might make fun of me

UE:   People might think less of me

UN:   People might not love me

CH:   I mustn't do anything silly

CB:   It would be social suicide to be silly

UA:   I might not be taken seriously

TH:   People will think I'm an idiot

EB:   Maybe there are times in my past

SE:   Where I acted silly

UE:   Or was made to feel silly

UN:   And people laughed at me

CH:   People got cross with me

CB:   People thought less of me

UA:   Maybe being silly got me into trouble

TH:   Maybe I vowed never to be silly again

EB:     And look where that's got me

SE:     Reading a book to increase my Happy

UE:     Maybe a bit of silliness is needed

UN:     Maybe a bit of silliness is OK

CH:     And who's the person deciding

CB:     Deciding what's silly and what's not

UA:     Is it more silly to be silly and happy

TH:     Or is it more silly to be serious all the time and unhappy


EB:     Maybe it's OK to be silly sometimes

SE:     Maybe it's OK to feel silly sometimes

UE:     I've felt silly in the past

UN:     And I survived 100% of the time


CH:     Maybe it's OK not to take myself so seriously

CB:     Maybe it's safe to feel silly

UA:     Maybe it's OK to try  new things

TH:     That might make me feel silly

EB:     Maybe I can choose to feel a different way

SE:     Maybe I can choose to feel happy

UE:     Maybe I can choose to feel curious about why I feel silly

UN:     Maybe I can choose to feel excited about trying something
new

CH:     Maybe I can choose to feel brave about trying something new

CB:     Maybe I can choose to feel silly about feeling silly

UA:     Maybe I can choose to not feel silly about feeling silly

TH:     Maybe it's entirely up to me


EB:     Isn't that an empowering thought

SE:     Or maybe it's a silly thought

UE:     And maybe it doesn't matter

UN:     Maybe I'm assuming it's silly

CH:     Maybe I'm assuming other people are judging me

CB:     Based on past experiences

UA:     Maybe I can let that go now

TH:     I choose to feel happy to let that go

# I'M NO GOOD AT ANYTHING

KC:   Even though I'm no good at anything, I choose to deeply and completely accept and honour myself

KC:   Even though I'm no good at anything, I choose to deeply and completely love and accept myself

KC:   Even though I don't think I'm good at anything, I have no talent, no potential, no promise, no skills – I choose to deeply and completely love and accept myself anyway. And maybe anyone else who taught me to think this.

EB:   I'm no good at anything

SE:   I'm no good at anything

UE:   I'm talentless

UN:   I have no skills

CH:   I'm no good at anything

CB:   I do everything badly

UA:   I know this

TH:     I know I'm no good at anything


EB:     I know because I've been told

SE:     Someone told me

UE:     Someone that I trust

UN:     Someone in a position of authority

CH:     Told me I was no good at anything

CB:     And I believed them

UA:     Why would they lie

TH:     It must be true


EB:     But just in case I mistakenly do well at something

SE:     I have to keep repeating to myself

UE:     What they told me

UN:     I'm no good at anything

CH:     I have to tell myself over and over

CB:     So I don't mistakenly think

UA:     That I AM good at something

TH:     Cos I'm no good at anything

EB:     What….anything?

SE:     Of all things in all the world

UE:     I'm no good at ANYTHING?

UN:     Nope

CH:     I'm pretty useless

CB:     Maybe I'm GOOD at being useless

UA:     Maybe I'm good at not being good at anything

TH:     Wait…


EB:     That can't be true because I'm no good at anything

SE:     Not even not being good at anything

UE:     I'm confused

UN:     Am I good at feeling confused?

CH:     I can't be cos I'm no good at anything

CB:     So am I confused or not

UA:     Can you be good at being confused?

TH:     If you can that's not me

EB:     And what's my standard for 'good'

SE:     What's my basis for comparison

UE:     How do I know I'm less good at something

UN:     Than everyone else in the entire world

CH:     Do I know everyone else in the entire world

CB:     How do I KNOW I'm no good at anything

UA:     Who told me

TH:     Or did I tell myself


EB:     How do I know

SE:     Where's my evidence that I'm no good at ANYTHING

UE:     Could it be that I'm generalizing

UN:     Why would I feel the need to tell myself

CH:     That I'm no good at anything

CB:     What am I afraid of

UA:     Am I afraid that actually I'm really good

TH:     What would that mean


EB:     If I was really good at something

SE:    What would I have to do

UE:    What would people say

UN:    Would they still love me

CH:    Would I lose friends if I was good at something

CB:    Would I have to push myself for a better job

UA:    A better life

TH:    That doesn't feel very safe


EB:    That would mean stepping out of my comfort zone

SE:    Better to convince myself

UE:    That I'm no good at anything

UN:    Maybe

CH:    I have skills and talents

CB:    Who am I not helping by not sharing these

UA:    Who am I helping by not sharing these

TH:    What am I afraid will happen if I'm good at something


EB:    I choose to acknowledge this fear

SE:    It's been trying to keep me safe

UE:    By keeping me small

UN:    I choose to let the fear go

CH:    I choose to know I am good at a lot of things

CB:    I choose to allow myself to get better at these

UA:    I choose to know it's safe to do so

TH:    I choose to feel happy about my pure potential

# I DON'T REALLY BELIEVE THAT (ACHIEVING A GOAL)

KC:    Even though I don't really believe that, I choose to be open to the possibility that it might be true

KC:    Even though I don't really believe that, I choose to be open to the possibility that it might be true whether I believe it or not

KC:    Even though I don't really believe that, I choose to be open to the possibility that I could

EB:    I don't really believe that

SE:    It seems a bit far fetched

UE:    I could never do that

UN:    I could never achieve that

CH:    I don't really believe I could

CB:    I might say I do

UA:    But I don't really

TH:    Not deep down

EB: It just doesn't seem possible

SE: I can't see HOW

UE: It feels too big

UN: Too unattainable

CH: It doesn't really feel true

CB: I can say or write these things

UA: But I don't really believe them

TH: I have that little voice


EB: "Yeah, but…"

SE: I don't really believe I can love myself

UE: I don't really believe I can appreciate myself

UN: I don't really believe I can be happy

CH: Because *[finish this sentence with WHY you don't believe you can be happy]*

CB: For that reason I can't be happy

UA: For that reason I can't achieve

TH: For that reason I don't really believe it if I say I can

EB:    And I got this reason from *[finish the sentence with WHO or WHAT or WHERE]*

SE:    So it must be true

UE:    And so I can't believe it

UN:    I can't allow myself to believe it

CH:    In case I get disappointed

CB:    In case it doesn't happen

UA:    Even if I believe it

TH:    That would be really upsetting


EB:    That would take away any hope

SE:    Better not to hope

UE:    Better not to get hurt

UN:    Better to not believe it

CH:    It's not safe to believe it

CB:    So I won't believe it

UA:    My little voice won't believe it

TH:    And I acknowledge that little voice

EB:    It's trying to keep me safe

SE:    But maybe by trying to keep me safe

UE:    It's telling me lies

UN:    Maybe I need to believe FIRST

CH:    Maybe nothing will happen without belief

CB:    Belief is very powerful

UA:    I believe I can't believe this

TH:    Is that really true?


EB:    Maybe I can believe

UE:    Maybe I can be open to believing

UN:    Maybe I can try believing on for size

CH:    I don't have to be stupid about it

CB:    But I could be open to it

UA:    I wonder what would happen if I was open to it

TH:    Maybe I could be open to finding out

# FEELING LIKE I'VE JUST DONE SOMETHING STUPID

KC:   Even though I feel like I've just done something stupid, I love and accept myself

KC:   Even though I feel like I've just done something really stupid and my stomach is in knots, I love and accept myself

KC:   Even though I'm really afraid that I've just done something stupid and I can't believe I allowed myself to do it, I deeply and completely love and accept myself

EB:   I feel like I've just done something stupid

SE:   It seemed like such a good idea at the time

UE:   I decided to be brave

UN:   And now I wish I hadn't

CH:   Cos I'm afraid of what will happen

CB:   Of how people will react

UA:   Of what they'll say

TH:  Why did I do it?!

EB:  My stomach is in knots about it

SE:  I wish I could wind back time

UE:  I have an overwhelming urge

UN:  To try to do some damage control

CH:  But I'm not even sure there IS damage

CB:  Of if I'm over reacting

UA:  What should I do

TH:  I'm feeling so stressed about it

EB:  I feel like I've just done something really stupid

SE:  Argh! Why did I do it?!

UE:  I wish I could take it back

UN:  All these knots in my stomach

CH:  What will they think

CB:  Have I made them uncomfortable

UA:  Have I embarrassed them

TH:  Have I embarrassed myself

EB: I can't believe I allowed myself to do it

SE: It's all going to go horribly wrong

UE: Not it's not, it'll be fine

UN: No it won't, I've just been really stupid

CH: Haven't I?

CB: Did I mean it with the best intentions

UA: Was I trying to be kind and supportive

TH: If yes, can it really be that stupid?


EB: What if I'm worrying for no reason

SE: What if I've panicked unnecessarily

UE: Who's the person who's decided what I did was stupid

UN: Me

CH: How do I KNOW it was stupid

CB: Or am I ASSUMING it might be stupid

UA: And just because I think it might be stupid

TH: It doesn't mean anyone else will

EB:     Maybe it's OK

SE:     Besides I've done it now

UE:     I have many talents

UN:     But time travel isn't one of them

CH:     Before I decided to panic and stress

CB:     Perhaps I can wait and see how it's received by others

UA:     Perhaps I'm just afraid they'll judge me

TH:     Perhaps they'd have judged me no matter what I did


EB:     Maybe that's their issue

SE:     I choose to feel OK

UE:     Feeling like I've done something stupid

UN:     I choose to be OK

CH:     Feeling like I've done something stupid

CB:     I choose to let the stress go

UA:     Feeling like I've done something stupid

TH:     I choose to relax


EB:     I choose to be calm

SE:     I choose to know I'm going to be OK

UE:     I choose to relax

UN:     I choose to be calm

CH:     I choose to let it be

CB:     I choose to let the panic go

UA:     I choose to let the worry go

TH:     I choose to feel OK

# CUSTOMISABLE TAPPING SCRIPT (FOR STRESS)

KC:   Even though I feel really stressed, I deeply and completely love and accept myself

KC:   Even though I feel really stressed because

_____, I deeply and completely love and accept myself.

KC:   Even though I feel really stressed and I feel it in my

_____ [*part of body*], I deeply and completely love and accept myself.

EB:   The truth is that I'm feeling really stressed

SE:   My nervous system is flooded with

_____*[the emotions you're feeling]*

UE:   And I really feel it

UN:   I don't want to feel it cos it's really uncomfortable

CH:   It feels really bad

CB:   No wonder I can't concentrate on anything

UA:    These emotions of _____ [the emotions you're feeling] are running through my nervous system

TH:    Over and over, I feel _____ *[the emotions you're feeling]*

EB:    I feel it in my _____ *[area of your body you feel it]*

SE:    All these terrible feelings of _____ *[the emotions you're feeling]*

UE:    I wonder how long I've been in this stress response?

UN:    I start thinking thoughts that feel really true to me

CH:    Thoughts like _____ *[what your Inner Voice is beating you up with, eg: I'm not good enough or I'm a loser]*

CB:    I think them over and over, on a loop

UA:    They feel really true and it really really hurts

TH:    These thoughts feel so true

EB:    And they always seem to get proved

SE:    So I say it over and over to myself _____ *[what your Inner Voice is beating you up with]*

UE:    And as I play those thoughts over and over in my head

UN:    I get more and more stressed and anxious

CH:    I get more and more _____ *[the emotions your feeling]*

TH:    This is a really vicious circle


EB:    No wonder I can't concentrate!

SE:    No wonder I feel so stuck!

UN:    No wonder I'm so full of self doubt!

CH:    I totally honour that my nervous system is flooding with these emotions

CB:     I totally honour that I'm reacting this way

UA:    I'm allowed to

TH:    Up to now it's been happening without me really realising


EB:    With me choosing

SE:    And I'm open to changing this now

UE:    I'm open to noticing what's happening

UN:    I'm open to realising how I'm reacting

CH:    And I'm open to changing this

CB:    I'm open to noticing and questioning this

UA:    I'm open to getting curious

TH:    Every time I feel and hear it come up


EB:    I'm open to re-wiring my nervous system for my highest good!

SE:    I'm open to re-wiring my pattern of behaviour for my highest good!

UE:    I'm open to a whole new way of thinking and acting and reacting!

UN:    I'm open to having a new choice about how I react!

CH:    Because when I shift…everything shifts!

CB:    Clearing out the old way that doesn't serve me

UA:    And inviting in a new and better way

TH:    Shifting into an empowered state of being


EB:    Shifting into empowered confidence

SE:    Saying YES to feeling calmer

UE:    Saying YES to feeling confident

UN:    Saying YES to taking inspired action

CH:    Saying YES to inspiration

CB:    Saying YES to motivation and excitement

UA:    Saying YES to being my most focused and productive self

TH:    Saying YES to SUCCESS!

Printed in Great Britain
by Amazon

17106700R00092